Growth Assessment in Childhood and Adolescence

D1196185

Growth Assessment in Childhood and Adolescence

CHARLES G. D. BROOK
MA MD FRCP DCH

*Consultant Paediatrician
and Paediatric Endocrinologist
The Middlesex Hospital
London*

Blackwell Scientific Publications
OXFORD LONDON EDINBURGH
BOSTON MELBOURNE

© 1982 by
Blackwell Scientific Publications
Editorial offices:
Osney Mead, Oxford OX2 0EL
8 John Street, London WC1N 2ES
9 Forrest Road, Edinburgh EH1 2QH
52 Beacon Street, Boston,
    Massachusetts 02108, USA
99 Barry Street, Carlton
    Victoria 3053, Australia

First published 1982

Set by Burns & Smith Ltd, Derby

Printed and bound in Great Britain by
Henry Ling Ltd, Dorchester

DISTRIBUTORS

USA
  Blackwell Mosby Book Distributors
  11830 Westline Industrial Drive
  St Louis, Missouri 63141

Canada
  Blackwell Mosby Book Distributors
  120 Melford Drive, Scarborough
  Ontario M1B 2X4

Australia
  Blackwell Scientific Book Distributors
  214 Berkeley Street, Carlton
  Victoria 3053

British Library
Cataloguing in Publication Data

Brook, Charles G.D.
  Growth assessment in childhood
    and adolescence
  1. Children—Growth
  I. Title
  612'.65   RJ 131
  ISBN 0-632-00955-1

Contents

Preface   vii

1   Prenatal Growth   1
2   Growth in Childhood   9
3   Tools of the Trade   29
4   The Small Child   53
5   The Tall Child   83
6   The Fat Child   96
7   The Thin Child   112
8   Puberty   120
9   Early Puberty   134
10 Late Puberty   144

Index   158

Preface

This book arises from my training with Professor J. M. Tanner, whose contribution to the study of human growth is unique. It is written in the belief that growth assessment makes such a major contribution to clinical paediatric practice that its principles should be widely available and employed by all workers in medicine and allied professions who have the care of the health of children. This book aims to put growth assessment — the basic skill of paediatrics — into the market place.

The philosophy of my paediatric practice owes much to the work and thoughts of Professor Tanner, Professor O.H. Wolff, Dr R. J. K. Brown and Dr Stephen Herman and I thank them for their unwitting help. Miss Lynette Napper started the secretarial grind which underlies the writing of a book: I am grateful for her help in getting things started but the major work has been that of Mrs Sue Shorvon whose unfailing cheerfulness in the face of my demands has made it all fun. I give her my very special thanks.

CHARLES G. D. BROOK
THE MIDDLESEX HOSPITAL 1982

CHAPTER 1

Prenatal Growth

Growth begins at conception and is at its fastest between conception and birth; because of this, the prenatal part of the growth process is the part most vulnerable to adverse environmental circumstances and the time when such circumstances have the most long-lasting and severe effects. Paradoxically, it is also the period about which we have least knowledge and on which we are least able to exert control. Nevertheless, advances in perinatal morbidity and mortality will only be achieved by a better understanding of what is going on at this time.

A principal reason for our lack of knowledge stems from lack of access to the normal fetus between the time when social abortions are performed and the time when normal babies are born. Advances in ultrasound have made a considerable difference to this situation and ultrasound is the most reliable method by which to bring an infant to delivery appropriately grown and with a normal growth potential following a gestation period of 40 weeks from the date of the last menstrual period. Unfortunately, a single late ultrasonic measurement is probably insufficient to detect poor growth and repeated measurements are needed (Ellis & Bennett 1981).

Measurements of crown–rump length by ultrasound indicate that fetal growth is exponential up to twelve weeks and thereafter linear (Campbell 1976, Birkbeck 1976). Crown–rump and crown–heel lengths increase proportionately in the early weeks although, as fetal age advances, the legs get disproportionately longer. Biparietal and occipitofrontal measurements of skull diameter correlate closely with measurements of length (Birkbeck 1976). Growth in length during the first trimester proceeds at a

1

sufficiently reliable rate to allow predictions of gestational age from a single determination of length at this time (Robinson 1973). Later, because length measurements become more difficult, skull diameter must be used, but this too provides reliable information on which to base an estimate of gestational age (Campbell & Newman 1971), always assuming that the pregnancy is a normal one.

Comparisons of measurements made by ultrasound (Robinson 1973) with actual measurements made on aborted fetuses (Birkbeck 1976) and with birth length standards (Lubchenko *et al* 1966) show remarkable agreement. Fig. 1.1 shows the growth curve of the human fetus and Fig. 1.2 the rate of growth in length during gestation drawn by me from these data. These are technically known as distance and velocity curves respectively.

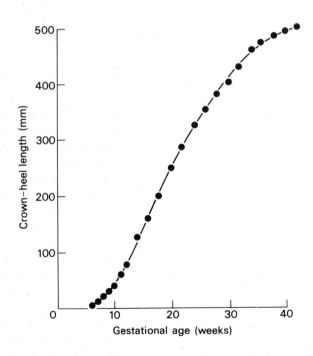

Fig. 1.1 Growth curve of human fetus.

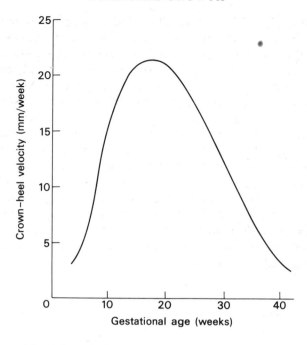

Fig. 1.2   Velocity curve of fetal growth in length.

Fetal weight gain naturally follows growth in length, but the peak velocity of weight gain occurs later than that of height because of the contribution made to weight by the various internal body organs. Of these, the brain is by far the biggest contributor, although its weight does have a significant relationship to other bodily dimensions (Jordaan 1976). Fetal body composition is relevant to the nursing of newborn infants: the increased water content of preterm babies together with their greater surface area: weight ratio and the fact that their skin readily loses water are all highly relevant. In this context, it is important to realise that the baby born at 32 weeks is not at all in the same situation two weeks later at a postmenstrual age of 34 weeks, as the baby just being born at 34 weeks. For this reason measurements of physiological functions made after birth have to take account of both gestational age and extrauterine age.

In spite of the fact that all babies are weighed at birth, it has to be admitted by any practising physician that this is done more or less by convention and because it is easier than measuring length, rather than because it produces useful information. The increased birthweight of the premature infant of the diabetic mother makes all the points necessary to indicate what a useless measurement weight is as an estimate of maturity or of fetal well being. In the newborn nursery day-to-day weight changes are useful because they are sufficient in magnitude to allow longitudinal estimates of growth to be made. I doubt, however, whether many babies would come to serious harm if routine weighing were abandoned in all but sick babies. Measurement of neonatal length is not difficult and an excellent instrument is available (Fig. 1.3, Davies & Holding 1972). Tape measurements of length are not worth making.

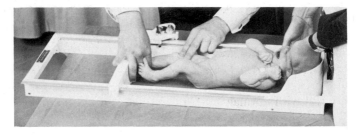

Fig. 1.3 Measuring length of a newborn with a Harpenden neonatometer. (Available from Holtain Ltd., Crosswell, Crymych, Dyfed SA41 3UF, Wales.)

Brain growth is, of course, by far the most important event of prenatal life. The relationship between the increase in head circumference and brain development in the normally growing infant during the first year of postnatal life is well established and probably holds for the intrauterine period as well (Brandt 1976). The major spurt in human brain growth begins in mid-pregnancy and brain cells continue to increase in number into the second postnatal year, myelination continuing the process still further into the third and fourth years (Dobbing 1976).

Even then, functional maturity is far from complete, as the increase in subsequent performance of children with late-treated hypothyroidism shows (Money *et al* 1978). The problem of studying brain growth is that structure and function may be quite separate. While the concept of the vulnerability of the developing brain is well accepted (Dobbing 1981), access to affected human material is severely restricted and extrapolations from animal material may be inappropriate.

Birth is incidental to the growth process as long as environmental circumstances within or without the uterus remain optimal. Because they often do not remain so and because this has effects on the growth of the baby, both birthweight (which is an indirect measure of birth length) and length of gestation are associated with perinatal mortality. To have the highest chance of surviving, an infant should be born between 38 and 41 weeks of gestation, weighing between 3400 and 4200 grams (Goldstein & Peckham 1976). Birth outside these ranges is associated with increased mortality and morbidity and antenatal care is directed at trying to achieve delivery of babies within these ranges as often as possible. The care of premature and small-for-dates infants seeks to optimise the environment and thus to maximise the chances of survival with normal function.

INFLUENCES ON FETAL GROWTH

Apart from sexual differentiation, *the fetal testis* causes a substantial difference between males and females in terms of size for a given postmenstrual age and males are always bigger than females. This applies both to primiparous and multiparous mothers and for infants of different races. From a practical point of view it is therefore important to use sex-specific standards when considering the growth of a newborn infant.

The contribution of *genetics* to fetal growth is probably not all that great. The correlation in birthweight between two successive siblings is in the order of 0.5 but much of this rather surprisingly low correlation must be due to maternal size. Height and mid-pregnancy weight affect birthweight and should be allowed for when comparing different infants (Tanner & Thomson 1970).

Nutrition before and during pregnancy may influence fetal growth. Clear-cut relationships are difficult to show in societies where obvious malnutrition is uncommon and diet variability considerable, but there are suggestions that minor degrees of subclinical malnutrition, especially of vitamins and trace metals, may contribute to the incidence of congenital malformation. The problem is that such relationships are at the limit of detection and much work needs to be done to establish whether supplementing the diets of pregnant women will improve the outcome of their pregnancies. When nutritional disasters occur, on the other hand, the effect on fetal growth is obvious (Stein & Susser 1975).

Obese women tend to have heavy infants and this is probably due to increased amounts of subcutaneous fat (Whitelaw 1976). Extreme obesity, because it represents a very abnormal situation in the mother, may lead to obstetric hazard and very high increments of maternal weight may lead to a decrease in the weight of the newborn (Curr 1962). Attempts are being made to develop equations for maternal measurements obtained at mid-pregnancy which will identify mothers carrying fetuses at risk from malnutrition. Such predictors of fetal growth should make a substantial improvement on perinatal morbidity (Metcalfe 1978).

Smoking is now well recognised to be an adverse fetal growth factor and the effects of smoking on subsequent learning ability and growth are alarming (Butler & Goldstein 1973). Whether such effects are caused by direct toxicity or by secondary effects on maternal behaviour is not clear, but there is no doubt that cessation of smoking in women of childbearing age would have a very definite beneficial effect on their offspring. Unfortunately for mothers-to-be, the balance of evidence is that drugs and alcohol and excessive ingestion of tea and coffee may also be found to be important when considering the production of perfect children.

Altitude above sea level may be important to fetal growth, although the influence of other factors, such as the size of the mother, has not yet been adequately explored. Interaction of socioeconomic factors with malnutrition, smoking, obesity and so on is exceedingly complex but what *is* certain is that the effects of poor environmental circumstances are probably more important to fetal growth than most of the influences which come within the remit of doctors to alter. This is unfortunately true of much of the promotion of child health: housing, nutrition and education are much more important than traditional medical care.

Hormonal factors are the principal modulators of the growth process and endogenous hormone production, placental, and maternal hormones are all important. The interchange of the feto–placental unit with the maternal endocrine system is of considerable relevance here and is poorly understood. At present we are at the stage of describing changing concentrations of hormones in infants, but as changes in receptors and in the catabolism of hormones are certainly equally important to mechanisms of hormone action, we are only at a qualitative and not very informed stage of understanding fetal endocrinology.

REFERENCES

BIRKBECK J. A. (1976) Metrical growth and skeletal development of the human fetus. In Roberts D. F. and Thomson A. M. (eds.) *The Biology of Human Fetal Growth* pp. 39-68. Taylor and Francis, London.

BRANDT I. (1976) Dynamics of head circumference growth before and after term. In Roberts D. F. and Thomas A. M. (eds.) *The Biology of Human Fetal Growth* pp. 109-136. Taylor and Francis, London.

BUTLER N. R. & GOLDSTEIN H. (1973) Smoking in pregnancy and subsequent child development. *British Medical Journal* 4, 573-5.

CAMPBELL S. (1976) Antenatal assessment of fetal growth and development. In Roberts D. F. and Thomson A. M. (eds.) *The Biology of Human Fetal Growth* pp.15-38. Taylor and Francis, London.

CAMPBELL S. & NEWMAN G. B. (1971) Growth of the fetal biparietal diameter during normal pregnancy. *Journal of Obstetrics and Gynaecology of the British Commonwealth* 78, 513-9.

CURR M. G. (1962) The problem of the overweight patient in pregnancy. *Journal of Obstetrics and Gynaecology of the British Commonwealth* **69**, 980–95.

DAVIES D. P. & HOLDING R. E. (1972) Neonatometer. A new infant length measurer. *Archives of Disease in Childhood* **47**, 938.

DOBBING J. (1976) Vulnerable periods in brain growth and somatic growth. In Roberts D. F. and Thomson A. M. (eds.) *The Biology of Human Fetal Growth* pp. 137–47. Taylor and Francis, London.

DOBBING J. (1981) The later development of the brain and its vulnerability. In Davis J. A. and Dobbing J. (eds.) *Scientific Foundation of Paediatrics,* 2nd ed. Heinemann, London.

ELLIS C. & BENNETT M. J. (1981) Detection of intrauterine growth retardation by ultrasound: preliminary communication. *Journal of the Royal Society of Medicine* **74**, 739–41.

GOLDSTEIN H. & PECKHAM C. (1976) Birthweight, gestation, neonatal mortality and child development. In Roberts D. F. and Thomson A. M. (eds.) *The Biology of Human Fetal Growth* pp. 80–102. Taylor and Francis, London.

JORDAAN H. V. F. (1976) Newborn brain: body weight ratios. *American Journal of Physical Anthropology* **44**, 279–84.

LUBCHENKO L. O., HAUSMAN C. & BOYD E. (1966) Intrauterine growth in length and head circumference as estimated from live births at gestational ages from 26 to 42 weeks. *Pediatrics* **37**, 403–8.

METCALFE J. (1978) Association of fetal growth with maternal nutrition. In Faulkener F. and Tanner J. M. (eds.) *Human Growth Vol. I: Principles and prenatal growth* pp. 415–60. Plenum Press, New York.

MONEY J., CLARKE F. C. & BECK J. (1978) Congenital hypothyroidism and IQ increase: a quarter century follow-up. *Journal of Pediatrics* **93**, 432–4.

ROBINSON H. P. (1973) Sonar measurement of fetal crown–rump length as means of assessing maturity in first trimester of pregnancy. *British Medical Journal* **4**, 28–31.

STEIN Z. & SUSSER M. (1975) The Dutch famine 1944–45 and the reproductive process. *Pediatric Research* **9**, 70–83.

TANNER J. M. & THOMSON A. M. (1970) Standards for birthweight at gestation periods from 32–42 weeks allowing for maternal height and weight. *Archives of Disease in Childhood* **45**, 566–9.

WHITELAW A. G. W. (1976) Influence of maternal obesity on subcutaneous fat in the newborn. *British Medical Journal* **1**, 985–6.

CHAPTER 2

Growth in Childhood

The growth curve of the human child has never been better exemplified than by the growth of the child of Count Philippe de Montbeillard between the years 1759 and 1777 (Tanner 1962). It is reproduced in Fig. 2.1. In the upper part of the figure, the heights of the child are plotted at six-monthly intervals against his chronological age, giving a distance curve; in the lower part increments over each six months are converted into annual rates and are plotted against chronological age to make a velocity curve. Growth in infancy is rapid but rapidly decelerating so that it describes an arc with a relatively short radius. The deceleration seen immediately after birth is a continuation of that seen in the fetal period and illustrated in Fig. 1.2 (p.3).

Between two and three years of age, the deceleration changes in magnitude and the years of middle childhood are years of steady and gradually decelerating growth, although there is a small increase in growth rate (possibly associated with the production of adrenal androgens (adrenarche)), and a discontinuation of deceleration, which has been called the mid-childhood growth spurt. This short-lived increase in growth rate, which can be clearly seen in Fig. 2.1, occurs mainly in boys and is the subject of study at present (Tanner & Cameron 1980). Overall, however, during the prepubcrtal years the growth curve assumes the shape of an arc with a relatively long radius. The slow deceleration is brought to an end by the adolescent growth spurt which rises to a peak and then disappears when epiphyseal fusion has been completed. The adolescent growth spurt adds approximately 20 cm to that of a boy, so the height at which puberty begins is important to the determination of final height.

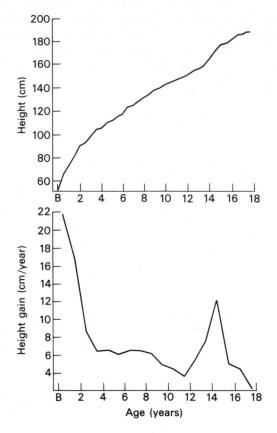

Fig. 2.1 Growth of the son of Count Philippe de Montbeillard, 1759–77. In the upper panel the height is plotted at six monthly intervals. In the lower panel the height increments over each successive six months are converted to annual rates and plotted against age. Reproduced with permission.

The growth of all children follows a curve similar to the one illustrated and, apart from deviations which are due to pathological processes, the spread in the height of growing children results from differences in genetic endowment of height and to differences in timing. Obviously the spread of normality increases as children get bigger, that is, they fan out, and those destined to be taller grow more quickly and vice versa. There is some rearrangement of ranking of birth lengths, but at every age the standard deviation of height distribution represents a relatively fixed percentage of the mean. The shapes of individual curves are remarkably uniform and the regularity of growth can be demonstrated by the ability to derive an equation containing only five parameters which describes growth in stature from age two until maturity (Preece & Baines 1978).

Boys grow a little faster than girls before puberty and gain about 1.5 cm in prepubertal growth but the major difference between the growth of boys and girls results from the difference in timing of the adolescent growth spurt. Fig. 2.2 is taken from the work of Largo and colleagues (1978), who analysed the adolescent growth

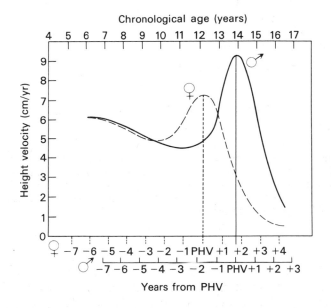

Fig. 2.2 The adolescent growth spurt in girls and boys. Peak height velocities (PHV) occurred at age 12 in girls and 14 in boys and the scale at the base of the figure indicates velocity measurements for years before and after PHV. (Data from Largo *et al* 1978). Reproduced with permission.

spurt from the data of the longitudinal study of growth in Zurich from 1955–1976. These workers found that the age at which the height velocity was at a minimum before the adolescent growth spurt began was 9.6 years in girls and 11.0 years in boys. Thus girls had a loss of 1.4 years of preadolescent growth at a rate of just under 5 cm per year, which accounted for 6.5 cm in adult height. This difference in timing increased to a difference of 1.7 years in the age at peak velocity, which girls achieved at an average of 12.2 years and boys at an average of 13.9 years.

Girls achieved their peak height velocity of adolescence of 7.1 cm per year in 2.6 years, whereas boys achieved their peak height velocity of adolescence of 9.0 cm per year over 2.9 years. Since the peak height velocity of adolescence was greater and later in boys than in girls, the area under the curve describing the adolescent growth spurt of the male was 2.3 times as great as the area under the curve of the adolescent growth spurt of the female. This accounted for a further 6.0 cm in the final adult heights of men and women.

The gain of 1.5 cm in prepubertal height, of 6.5 cm in a later take-off of the growth spurt, and of 6.0 cm in the magnitude and duration of the growth spurt would lead to an adult height difference between the sexes of 14.0 cm. In fact, the final height of the average man in the Zurich study was 177.4 cm and of the average woman 164.8 cm — a difference of 12.6 cm at the mean — and this is due to the fact that females grow rather more than males after the peak height velocity of adolescence has been achieved. The adult sex difference of height (12.6 cm) is extremely important in growth assessement.

These mean figures conceal enormous individual variation. Thus the range of age at peak height velocity was 9.3 to 15.0 years in girls and 12.0 to 15.8 years in boys in the Zurich study. The variation in the duration of the adolescent growth spurt and in the height of its peak was also extremely striking: growth at adolescence may last for as little as 1.3 years in girls and 2.6 years in boys, or may exceed six and eight years respectively. The difference between prepubertal height velocity at its minimum and the peak height velocity during adolescence may be as little as 0.7 cm per year in girls and 1.9 cm in boys, or as large as 5.6 and 7.7 cm per year respectively. Consequently, while mean heights, velocities, and ages tell us something about human growth in general terms, they are of little help in individual cases.

Some details of the Zurich study differ quantitatively from the other major study of the adolescent growth spurt (Tanner *et al* 1976), but qualitatively they show considerable concordance. In the Tanner study, relationships were examined with the development of secondary sex characteristics. The appearance of pubic hair and breasts were significantly correlated with the age at onset and peak of the adolescent growth spurt, but they were independent of chronological age and of height achieved in prepuberty. There were, however, two compensating mechanisms between the prepubertal and pubertal periods. A child with a late growth spurt tends to grow more slowly in the prepubertal period. A child who is small in relation to his adult height in prepuberty has a spurt which lasts longer than that of a child who is relatively taller in prepuberty. These compensatory mechanisms are of considerable relevance to the management of delayed growth.

The growth curves of other organs in the body vary considerably. Brain weight obtains approximately 80% of its adult size by the age of three but the main growth spurt runs from mid-pregnancy to about 18 months of postnatal age (Dobbing 1981). Although the growth spurt takes place across the perinatal period, which means that exposure to adverse environmental circumstances is dangerous at this time, it is remarkable clinically how resistant the brain is to perinatal insult, in spite of the fact that the period around birth is one of intense development of dendritic trees. We may not yet know how to look properly at the problems occurring at this stage of development and their later effects. On the other hand, adult neuronal cell number is accomplished at an earlier (safer) time and myelination comes later, again at a safer, postnatal, time. In terms of growth assessment, biparietal diameter is what is measured in the fetus and occipitofrontal diameter is used to assess brain growth after birth, both reflecting brain size. Fig. 2.3 shows the distance and velocity curves of head circumferential growth in childhood.

Body fat has a growth curve all of its own. Fig. 2.4 shows the log sum of the 50th centile values of triceps and subscapular skinfold thicknesses for boys and girls plotted against chronological age (data from Tanner & Whitehouse 1975). Body fat increases rapidly during the first year of life in both sexes and achieves a peak which is slightly greater and slightly later in boys than in girls. In prepuberty skinfold thicknesses decrease, but as the whole body size is increasing the total amount of body fat remains about the same, being spread more thinly. In boys

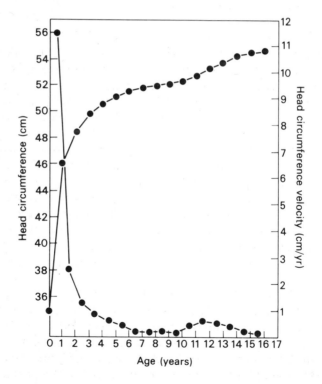

Fig. 2.3 Distance and velocity curves of head circumference growth in childhood.

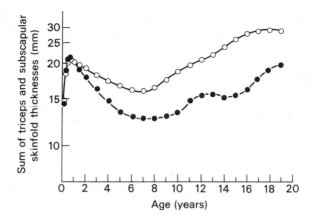

Fig. 2.4 Growth of body fat. Changes in skinfold thickness with age in childhood. ● Boys, ○ girls.

there is an increase in skinfold thickness which precedes the other changes of puberty but in both sexes, fat increases in puberty, although much more so in girls than in boys. There is also a redistribution of fat which leads to a loss of limb fat in boys and a marked accumulation of trunk fat in both sexes.

These changes in distribution have been little researched and could well be helpful in the clinical situation as they seem to precede other changes of puberty and can be used as heralding the main events. Body fat increases and changes in distribution during the whole of adult life and only diminishes in the sixth and seventh decades (Hawk 1978). The adipose organ certainly has the longest growth process and the one most susceptible to environmental influence.

Finally, have we any way by which we can make allowance for individual differences in the timing of the various events which comprise the growth process? For many years it had been assumed that skeletal maturation might help, but Marshall (1974) investigated the interrelationships of skeletal maturation with sexual development and somatic growth. Broadly speaking, the age at which puberty is entered is not more closely tied to skeletal age than it is to chronological age. Nor does skeletal age help in predicting what will happen to growth at adolescence. It does, however, have a more direct relationship than does chronological age with the percentage of growth that has been completed. For this reason it is helpful in the prediction of final height and of considerable importance in growth assessment. It will be further considered in Chapter 3.

MODULATORS OF THE GROWTH PROCESS

Timing

Differences in the timing of growth make a substantial contribution to within-culture differences between children. In terms of stature, children of the same age attending the same school have a normal height range of over 20 cm. The tallest and the smallest have a very different outlook on life, which may or may not impinge on their performance in school and on their relationships with others. Much of this variation will be genetically determined, but a considerable amount of it will be due to differences in the timing of the growth process. What controls timing is obscure. There is often a family history of late maturing in cases of delayed growth, but quite often there is not and there are no studies which have systematically examined relationships in timing between generations. What is needed is for the children of parents who were themselves subjects in one of the longitudinal growth studies to be followed through their own growth and puberty.

The mechanisms which underlie the timing of the events of growth are poorly understood and we are in the position of observational astronomers in this respect. We can forecast in individual cases more or less what is going to happen from what has happened already, but we cannot tell a parent at conception how the growth of his individual child will proceed.

Genetic influences

Racial differences play an obvious part in determining the variation of human growth and standards of growth are available from many countries (Eveleth & Tanner 1976). In clinical terms, relatively little is known about the effects on growth of being reared in a different culture. A study in our hospital has shown that babies of Indian mothers born in north-west London are about 300 g lighter than their Caucasian equivalents at term; 15% of Indian babies were below the 5th centile for British standards and West Indian babies fell between their Indian and British peers (Grundy *et al* 1978). The consequences of these data for health administration in terms of special care facilities and staffing ratios are poorly researched and little recognised.

The largest differences in height between races are due to shape: Chinese people have short legs, Africans long legs, etc. Timing of growth between races probably does play a part and in clinical practice it is wise to be alive to this possibility but, taken as a whole, my personal experience is to find more within-race than between-race variation. Thus, while it may be desirable to have appropriate growth standards for the population with which one is dealing (Goldstein & Tanner 1980), there is little evidence that growth potential is much affected by ethnic differences (Waterlow 1980). For this reason it is justifiable to use growth standards from developed countries internationally, especially when, as will become clear, the essential prerequisite for proper growth assessment is the measurement of the rate of growth. Ideal rates of growth vary relatively little between different populations.

With the completion of longitudinal surveys we are beginning to see the emergence of data on two aspects of growth, first on the relationships between relatives and secondly, on the effects of growth in childhood on adult measurements. Hitherto, for want of data, much reliance has been placed on twin studies to assess the contribution of genetic influences to the growth process. Our own experience of estimating the effects of genetic and environmental influences on body fatness has shown how misleading this can be.

Of all characteristics, body fatness can be observed to run in families. The question is whether this is the effect of genes or environment. Our studies (Brook *et al* 1975, Hawk & Brook 1979b) came to diametrically opposed conclusions: when we considered twin data alone, we showed a massive genetic contribution to the determination of body fatness in childhood, but the addition of data from parents and siblings indicated that this must have been largely the result of subjecting monozygotic twins to a more similar environment than dizygotic twins. In the determination of a characteristic by environmental factors, monozygotic twins have a spuriously high correlation because they share a more common environment than dizygotic twins (Smith 1965). We learned a salutary lesson and there seems little doubt that body fatness is a characteristic which is largely environmentally determined.

The genetic contribution to the variation in height appears to be greater. For a characteristic which is 100% genetically determined, the regression coefficient of the value for the characteristic in the adult offspring plotted against midparent values will be 1.0, since offspring share all their genes in common with their parents; the regression coefficient of the mid-parental value plotted against that of the offspring is 0.5 since half the genes are in common. Since a correlation coefficient is the geometrical mean of these regression coefficients, the theoretical correlation coefficients between the measurement of a characteristic between two parents and their adult offspring for 100% genetic determination is thus $\sqrt{0.5 \times 1.0} = 0.71$.

Our data from England (Hawk & Brook 1979b) and those from other sources (Belgian and Swiss: Susanne 1975, and Brook *et al* 1977) showed correlation coefficients for adult height which approached this theoretical value. It is, therefore, hardly surprising to find that one can reliably predict adult height from childhood values (Hawk & Brook 1979a), whether or not one adds skeletal maturity and perhaps even parental heights, as maybe one should in the best of worlds (Bayley & Pinneau 1952, Tanner *et al* 1975). Quite the reverse is true for body fatness, which is largely environmentally determined and for which adult values cannot accurately be predicted from childhood ones (Hawk & Brook 1979a, 1979b). Body weight, being an amalgam, falls between the two extremes.

Environmental influences

Environmental influences on the growth process depend upon their magnitude, their duration, and also upon how fast growth should actually be occurring. An environmental insult, especially one which is prolonged or severe and particularly if it comes during a period of rapid growth, leads to damage to the growth process which is irrecoverable. This is why early intervention to improve a poor growth rate is essential for a satisfactory outcome.

Nutrition

Food is essential for growth and during consideration of the causes of poor growth, aspects of nutrition continually arise. During the intrauterine period, the effects of long continued poor intrauterine growth can be seen in low birthweight and short birth length, neither of which probably recover completely after birth. An acute period of intrauterine starvation may lead to fetal death but catch-up growth may well occur subsequently. Fig. 2.5 makes the point that it is possible to become light-for-dates in two very different ways and the data of Fancourt *et al* (1976) of low birthweight infants followed up subsequently makes the point with regard to the consequences of intrauterine malnutrition (Table 2.1).

The same principle can apply also in extrauterine life. Fig. 2.6 depicts the progress of two infants admitted to hospital with a similar weight at four months of age. Both demonstrated gross failure to thrive, but whereas one (R.L.) had been acutely starved by his psychotic mother, the other (H.C.) was the victim of civil strife in the Vietnam war over the complete four months of his life.

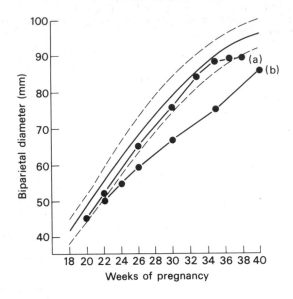

Fig. 2.5 The two ways of becoming small-for-dates: a) by acute starvation, b) by prolonged malnutrition in utero.

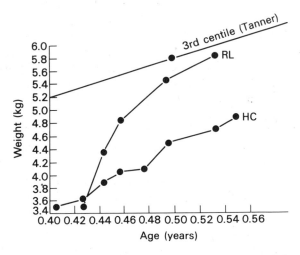

Fig. 2.6 The effect on subsequent catch-up growth of prolonged postnatal malnutrition (HC) compared with acute starvation (RL).

Table 2.1 Height centiles of low birthweight children at a mean age of four years.

	Less than 10th	10–50th	50–90th
Prolonged intrauterine starvation	14	17	
Acute placental failure	2	17	10

Data from Fancourt *et al* (1976)

R.L. regained weight rapidly on a re-feeding regimen but even a very large calorie intake could not induce catch-up growth in the case of H.C.

In this context it must be remembered that most children, at least in relatively affluent communities, receive a considerable excess of food. It is possible to grow at a normal rate with what is apparently a very low food intake and many are the consultations for children whose food intake does not meet parental expectations and yet who are perfectly normal. Because of the increase in growth rate which is seen around puberty, the growth process once again becomes particularly vulnerable to poor nutrition and mild degrees of anorexia may cause blunting of the puberty growth spurt and sometimes arrest of puberty. This is not a rare problem and is particularly common in poorly treated asthmatic children and in diabetic children having problems with control.

Overnutrition also affects growth. Increased nutrition at a period of rapid growth appears to increase growth rate but this is compensated by an overall shortening of the whole growth process by bone age advance (Brook 1973). Thus, obese (tall) children have normal heights for bone age and do not become tall adults (Lloyd *et al* 1961).

Emotional climate

It is often difficult to separate the effects of socioeconomic circumstances (which include nutritional problems) from the direct effects of emotional stress. Further, once a child

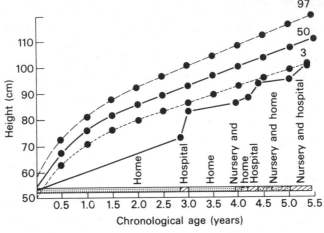

Fig. 2.7 The effect of an adverse home environment on growth in childhood.

is short, the emotional consequences of being short may be considerable. There are, however, well documented cases of emotional environment being the cause of severe growth retardation and Fig. 2.7 exemplifies one such case where deductive methodology leads to the inevitable conclusion that the child grows badly whenever the home is part of his environment. The consequences of this sort of emotional deprivation are also seen in mental development and cases such as this one represent to me clear examples of non-accidental injury. In practice, it proves extremely difficult to persuade those who will be galvanised into action by a single fracture to take this much more serious evidence of baby battering with the same degree of concern. Adverse socioeconomic circumstances are undoubtedly foremost in the determination of short stature, at least in the United Kingdom (Lacey & Parkin 1974), and any child who thrives in a hospital environment should be regarded with the highest suspicion in this respect. Overall, the measurement of the children's growth in a society acts as a barometer of overall national well being but few countries (Cuba being a notable exception (Jordan *et al* 1975)) have established programmes for the monitoring of child health in this way.

Seasonal variation

Seasons of the year used to be thought to play a major part in growth, but Marshall's painstaking studies (1975) showed that only about one-third of children have cycles of velocity which are seasonal. Nevertheless, rates of growth do vary considerably during the year and, in his fastest quarter, a child may grow at three times the rate of his slowest. Great care needs to be exercised in interpreting growth rates measured over less than a whole year.

Exercise

Inactivity is certainly harmful to bone growth but whether an increased level of physical activity is beneficial is not known (Bailey *et al* 1978). Experimental data may suggest that increased physical activity leads to a greater density of bone but the influence of activity is clearly multifactorial, since exercise affects muscle growth (mainly cell size) and is a potent stimulator of various hormones, notably growth hormone. Further, physical prowess is so strongly affected by a child's general physique that it is difficult to know whether healthy children are naturally active or whether their activity actually promotes their health. Certainly, there is a little evidence that strenuous training regimens improve physical growth and it is not likely that increasing exercise will actually improve growth since young athletes are comparable in growth status and development to non-athletes.

Endocrine influences

Although there is much speculation, there are few hard data on the hormonal contributions to prenatal growth. Observation of children with disorders of growth indicates that endocrine influences are extremely important in modulating postnatal growth. Considerable increase in knowledge has arisen through the availability of techniques to measure concentrations of hormones, but as yet the influences of hormone binding in blood, of the generation of receptor sites for hormone action and of the catabolic rates of hormones have been little investigated.

No single hormone alone modulates growth. The growth-stopping effect of an absence of thyroxin is probably more profound than that of any other hormone, including growth hormone, but the growth process requires interaction of these with many if not all other hormones. Although we know a little of what is responsible for the rapid growth of puberty, we do not yet understand how the rapid growth in infancy gives way to the slowly decelerating growth of middle childhood.

Growth hormone (GH) has few direct effects, if any: secretion by the pituitary gland is thought to be a response to a hypothalamic signal which is not yet established, and it leads to the generation of a family of peptides from the liver, and possibly from other tissues, which are collectively called somatomedins (Holder & Preece 1981). The terminology is difficult in this rapidly evolving field and the following substances — which are GH dependent, possess insulin-like actions in extraskeletal tissues, and promote the incorporation of sulphate into cartilage — qualify as somatomedins: somatomedin A, somatomedin C, insulin-like growth factor (formerly called non-suppressible insulin-like activity) and multiplication stimulating activity. Some of these substances may turn out to have identical structures and exactly what they do is still far from clear, since instances of their lack are not common. They probably have an important regulatory function on GH secretion.

Such secretion is intermittent, although synthesis of GH is continuous. GH is stored in secretory granules in the somatotrophic cells of the anterior lobe of the pituitary gland. It is released in response to a variety of stimuli both physiological (deep sleep, physical exercise, stress and food) and pharmacological (insulin, glucagon, aminoacids, L-dopa, etc.). Suppression of GH secretion is probably brought about by that seemingly universal suppressor of hormone release, somatostatin. This tetradecapeptide, originally thought to be a specific growth hormone-release inhibiting hormone, is widely distributed throughout the body. It is certainly not specific to growth hormone and is one of the hormones of the paracrine system (hormones which are secreted and have their action locally). Another example is the antimüllerian hormone secreted by the fetal testis, which locally supresses müllerian structures in male fetal sexual differentiation.

GH levels are highest during puberty and are lower in childhood than they are in the newborn period. Levels in childhood are generally higher than in adults, in whom they are higher in females than in males. In both sexes there is a tendency for GH levels to decline with advancing age. The effect of sex steroids on GH is probably complicated by their action on somatomedin generation and reception but testosterone certainly seems to act synergistically with growth hormone in the male pubertal growth spurt (Aynsley-Green *et al* 1976). Low levels of oestrogen probably stimulate growth but high levels inhibit it, probably by an action on somatomedin generation. Sex steroids are capable of increasing the responsiveness of the growth hormone-releasing mechanisms to various stimuli. This is important in the clinical assessment of short children and will be considered in Chapter 4.

Insulin plays a complex role in growth as can be seen from the effects of early overnutrition. There are some reasons for supposing that insulin may have to do with the growth of the size of cells, whereas GH may have more to do with cell number. Both are necessary for growth, as clinical practice shows.

Prolactin shares many of the aminoacid residues in common with GH but it does not seem to have a clearly defined role in regulating growth. What may well be important is its stimulation of the production of 1,25-dihydroxycholecalciferol by the kidney. This hormone promotes calcium absorption and must be present for the absorption of sufficient calcium for bone growth.

Thyroid hormones increase overall rates of protein synthesis and turnover and there is certainly synergism between thyroxin and growth hormone. Curiously, considering the vital role which thyroid hormones play, much less is known about how they bring about their action.

The role of *sex hormones* is extremely important and again relatively little understood. After the newborn period, levels of the gonadal steroids fall fairly rapidly and are low during childhood. Around the age of 6–8 years, the adrenal gland begins to produce androgens, probably from the zona reticularis. Exactly how this is brought about (possibly by a change primarily in the adrenal gland or by an as yet unidentified adrenal androgen-stimulating hormone) is not known, but the rise is consistent in individual children, although the actual magnitude of adrenal androgen production seems to vary considerably. What physiological role this so-called adrenarche plays is quite unknown, but it may serve to entrain subsequent hormonal events of puberty.

In the adult, *pituitary gonadotrophins,* which are secreted in response to production of the hypothalamic decapeptide gonadotrophin-releasing hormone (GNRH), maintain the production of the gonadal steroids, spermatogenesis, and ovulation. Although sensitive assays for GNRH in peripheral blood have not yet been successfully employed, there seems good reason to suppose that GNRH is secreted continuously in small bursts. The well known changes of gonadotrophins, especially with the menstrual cycle, are modulated at pituitary level. Much debate surrounds how the relatively quiescent gonadotroph becomes the actively secreting cell in adult life. The consensus of opinion is now that the rate of secretory bursts of GNRH is critical to gonadotrophin synthesis and secretion, and that the changing in periodicity and size of the signal is probably responsible for the production of gonadotrophins that bring about the gonadal changes of puberty.

The relationship of the growth spurt to these changes is not fully understood. Growth hormone and the sex hormones act together, certainly in boys, and the low level of oestrogens in early puberty in girls is probably important for the growth spurt then. Whether increasing oestrogen concentrations are responsible for the final waning of the female adolescent growth spurt is not yet clear. The final phase of growth, which is so important to the acquisition of adult stature, is a complex interaction of all the endocrine influences.

REFERENCES

AYNSLEY-GREEN A., ZACHMANN M. & PRADER A. (1976) Interrelation of the therapeutic effects of growth hormone and testosterone on growth in hypopituitarism. *Journal of Pediatrics* **89**, 992-9.

BAILEY D. A., MALINA R. M. & RASMUSSEN R. C. (1978) The influence of exercise, physical activity and athletic performance on the dynamics of human growth. In Falkner F. & Tanner J. M. (eds.), *Human Growth* pp. 475-505. Plenum Press, New York.

BAYLEY N. & PINNEAU S. R. (1952) Table for predicting adult height from skeletal age revised for use with the Greulich Pyle hand standards. *Journal of Pediatrics* **40**, 423-41. (Erratum **41**, 371).

BROOK C. G. D. (1973) Fat Children. *British Journal of Hospital Medicine* **10**, 30-3.

BROOK C. G. D., GASSER T., WERDER E. A. *et al* (1977) Height correlations between parents and mature offspring in normal subjects and in subjects with Turner's, Klinefleter's and other syndromes. *Annals of Human Biology* **4**, 17-22.

BROOK C. G. D. HUNTLEY R. M. C. & SLACK J. (1975) Influence of heredity and environment in the determination of skinfold thickness in children. *British Medical Journal* **2**, 719-21.

DOBBING J. (1981) The later development of the brain and its vulnerability. In Davis J. A. & Dobbing J. (eds.), *Scientific Foundations of Paediatrics,* 2nd ed. Heinemann, London.

EVELETH P. B. & TANNER J. M. (1976) *Worldwide variation in human growth.* Cambridge University Press, London.

FANCOURT R., CAMPBELL S., HARVEY D. *et al* (1976) Follow-up study of small-for-dates babies. *British Medical Journal.* **1**, 1435-7.

GOLDSTEIN H. & TANNER J. M. (1980) Ecological considerations in the creation and the use of child growth standards. *Lancet* I, 582—5.

GRUNDY M. F. B., HOOD J. & NEWMAN G. B. (1978) Birthweight standards in a community of mixed racial origin. *British Journal of Obstetrics and Gynaecology* **85**, 481-6.

HAWK L. J. (1978) *Determinants of body fatness.* MD Thesis, University of Edinburgh.

HAWK L. J. & BROOK C. G. D. (1979a) Influence of body fatness in childhood on fatness in adult life. *British Medical Journal* **1**, 151-2.

HAWK L. J. & BROOK C. G. D. (1979b) Family resemblances of height, weight and body fatness. *Archives of Disease in Childhood* **54**, 877-9.

HOLDER A. T. & PREECE M. A. (1981) The somatomedins. In Brook C. G. D. (ed.) *Clinical Paediatric Endocrinology* pp. 96-112. Blackwell Scientific Publications, Oxford.

JORDAN J,, RUBEN M. HERNANDEZ J. *et al* (1975) The 1972 Cuban national child growth study as an example of population health monitoring: design and methods. *Annals of Human Biology* **2**, 153-71.

LACEY K. A. & PARKIN J. M. (1974) The normal short child. Community study of children in Newcastle upon Tyne. *Archives of Disease in Childhood* **49**, 417-24.

LARGO R. H., GASSER T., PRADER A. *et al* (1978) Analysis of the adolescent growth spurt using smoothing spline functions. *Annals of Human Biology* **5**, 421-34.

LLOYD J. K., WOLFF O. H. & WHELAN W. S. (1961) Childhood obesity — a longterm study of height and weight. *British Medical Journal* **2**, 145-8.

MARSHALL W. A. (1974) Interrelationships of skeletal maturation, sexual development and somatic growth in man. *Annals of Human Biology* **1**, 29-40.

MARSHALL W. A. (1975) The relationship of variations in children's growth rates to seasonal climatic variations. *Annals of Human Biology* **2**, 243-50.

PREECE M. A. & BAINES M. J. (1978) A new family of mathematical models describing the human growth curve. *Annals of Human Biology* **5**, 421-34.

SMITH R. T. (1965) A comparison of socio-environmental factors in monozygotic and dizygotic twins. Testing an assumption. In Vandenberg S. G. (ed.), *Methods and Goals in Human Behaviour Genetics*, pp. 45-61. Academic Press, New York.

SUSANNE C. (1975) Genetic and environmental influence on morphological characteristics. *Annals of Human Biology* **2**, 279-88.

TANNER J. M. (1962) *Growth at adolescence,* 2nd edn. Blackwell Scientific Publications, Oxford.

TANNER J. M. & CAMERON N. (1980) Investigation of the mid-growth spurt in height, weight and limb circumferences in single-year velocity data from the London 1966-67 growth survey. *Annals of Human Biology* **7**, 565-77.

TANNER J. M. & WHITEHOUSE R. H. (1975) Revised standards for triceps and subscapular skinfolds in British children. *Archives of Disease in Childhood* **50**, 142-5.

TANNER J. M., WHITEHOUSE R. H., MARSHALL W. A. *et al* (1975) *Assessment of Skeletal maturation and prediction of adult height.* Academic Press, New York. Also in *Archives of Disease in Childhood* (1975) **50**, 14-26. (Erratum in *Annals of Human Biology*, 1978 **5**, 491-2.)

TANNER J. M., WHITEHOUSE R. H., MARUBINI E. *et al* (1976) The adolescent growth spurt of boys and girls of the Harpenden growth survey. *Annals of Human Biology* **3**, 109-26.

WATERLOW J. C. (1980) Child growth standards. *Lancet* I, 71-2.

CHAPTER 3

Tools of the Trade

Measurement is the basis of growth assessment and anthropometric measurements are not difficult to perform. They do, however, like all measurements, require attention to detail in order to minimise error. This is important because single measurements are very much less helpful than repeated ones over a period of time. Since the errors of measurement are cumulative over each occasion, measurements done by different people using different techniques on different occasions lead to considerable difficulties in accurately assessing rates of growth. For this reason, many of the measurements that are regularly made in paediatric clinics are of little use in growth assessment beyond gaining an overall impression, whereas a little attention to detail would render them an invaluable record of child health.

Height

For children under two years of age, supine length should be measured and Figs. 1.3 (p. 4) and 3.1 show such measurements being performed using appropriate equipment for newborn babies and small children. For children over the age of two standing measurements are required and for this purpose a stadiometer should be employed (Fig. 3.2). In all instances the aim is to record the distance between flat surfaces applied to the top of the head and soles of the feet. Because heads vary in shape, a standard position of the skull is routinely used: the outer canthus of the eye should be in the same horizontal plane as the external auditory meatus. In all instances, gentle traction is applied to eliminate postural changes. There are changes in length as the day goes on but in practice, as

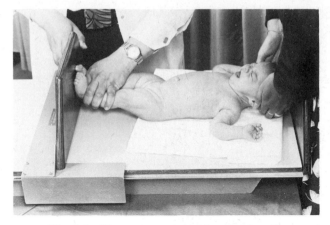

Fig. 3.1   The measurement of supine length.

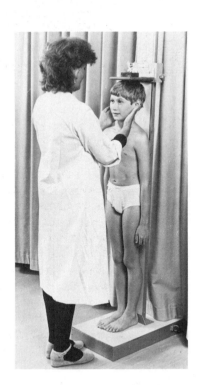

Fig. 3.2
The measurement of
standing height with a
stadiometer.

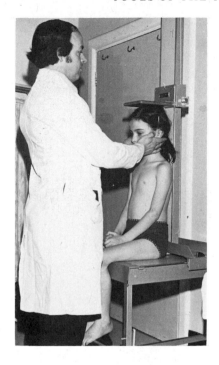

Fig. 3.3
The measurement of
sitting height.

most children will be measured in clinics which occur at the
same time of day on each occasion, the diurnal variation of
stature is not of great clinical significance.

The techniques of measuring are not difficult and can be
learned by any sympathetic person with a care for the
accuracy of the result of the measurement. A certain
amount of patience is needed in order to gain a child's co-
operation but with these provisos accurate measurements
are not difficult to come by.

In the assessment of short children, the measurement of
upper and lower body segments can be considerably
helpful. The use of span or pubis-to-ground measurements
is not recommended because of the difficulty in making an
accurate assessment. Measurements of sitting height (Fig.
3.3) and of crown-rump length in infants are to be greatly
preferred.

Most of the anthropometric instruments used in clinical practice have digital counter displays. These counters greatly reduce observer instrument errors but they do mean that there is no direct reading of each measurement. At the beginning of each clinic therefore, the accuracy of the machine must be checked. This can be done by use of a minimum reading on some instruments or by the use of a standard length on others. In my clinics, I tend to use myself as the easiest check that the digital counter is reading appropriately. When they go wrong, the counters give readings which are so ridiculous as to be immediately identifiable.

Weight

Measurements of weight are useful as an approximation to growth when the latter is very rapid. Thus, in the newborn nursery, measurements of weight are a valuable indicator of good health. The older a child becomes, the less value is weight or even weight change over a period of time as a measurement of growth. To be of any use, measurements of weight have to be recorded accurately on proper equipment and beam scales are the only acceptable instruments for use in this respect. A single measurement of weight is of very little help and other measures of the adequacy of nutrition are much more useful. Particular attention needs to be drawn to the fact that children gain only about 17 kg between the ages of two and ten, a velocity of less than 2 kg per year. Compared to height, the variations in weight during the day are enormous due to water balance and when this is taken with the use of inaccurate spring weighing scales, the undesirability of using weight as an estimate of children's growth becomes immediately apparent.

Assessment of nutrition

If an accurate assessment of fatness is required, skinfold thicknesses are easy to measure. These are much more helpful than attempting to compute weight-for-height indices in childhood. Fat and height are not gained at the same times, so indices which relate weight and height have different meanings at each age. In individual instances they may be misleading at best.

Skinfold thicknesses are measured by picking up a fold of skin and subcutaneous fat in a standard position, usually over the mid-point of the triceps muscle and under the scapula at 45° to the spine. The jaws of the skinfold caliper are applied and the needle of the dial of the instrument falls rapidly and then, suddenly, very slowly. The measurement of skinfold thickness should be recorded at that moment (Fig. 3.4). By convention the left side of the body is always used for anthropometric measurements but, if the child has an obvious deformity such as a hemiplegia, it is better to use the other side. In babies it is worth measuring both sides of the body and taking the average value for skinfold thicknesses (Whitelaw 1976).

The use of circumferential measurements (Fig. 3.5) is a variation in the assessment of nutrition. Such measures offer a less pure assessment of fatness, since a limb circumferential measurement measures not only fatness

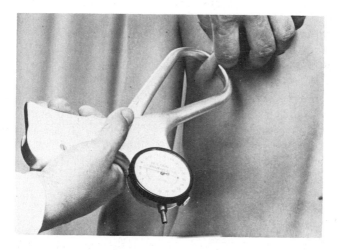

Fig. 3.4 The measurement of subscapular skinfold thickness with a Holtain skinfold caliper.

but also the amount of bone and muscle present, but in particular cases, they can be very helpful (e.g. in the clinical management of eating disorders) over a period of time. They are the only way of assessing head growth and the accurate measurement of head circumference (Fig. 3.6) is extremely useful in child developmental assessment. As so often is the case, the equipment provided for making such measurements is inadequate: the use of linen, plastic or paper tape measures makes the value of longitudinal measurements much less satisfactory than the use of a proper metal tape measure of the type shown. Here there is sufficient length on the end of the tape to make the reading of the circumference easy and it is thin enough not to slide about. All these instruments are available from Holtain Ltd., Crosswell, Crymych, Dyfed, SA41 3UF, Wales, or from Siber Hegner, Talstrasse, Zürich, Switzerland. The metallic tape is the Micromatic manufactured by Mabo Stanley of France and is widely available. Other anthropometric instruments are also available, specifically for measuring limb lengths and other body proportions but they are largely for research use.

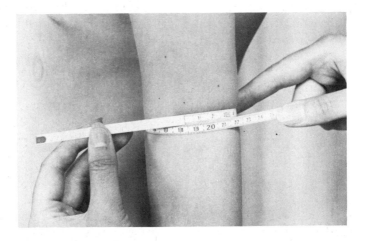

Fig. 3.5 The measurement of arm circumference.

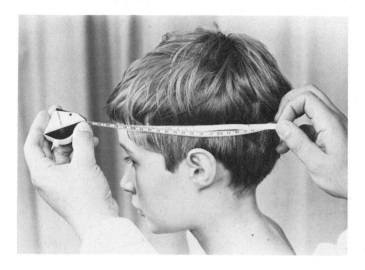

Fig. 3.6 The measurement of occipitofrontal circumference.

Standards

As a result of the pioneering work of Tanner and Whitehouse, standards are available for all the anthropometric measurements that have been discussed. Charts are available from Castlemead Publications, Castlemead, Hertford, SG14 1LM, England, and a useful reference book is also available (Buckler 1979) which contains all the relevant information.

Generally, standards are presented in terms of centiles, which describe the variation of a characteristic in a population. Where such a characteristic is distributed in a normal (gaussian) fashion, centile values correspond to the standard deviations in the populations (Fig. 3.7). Thus 68% of the population have a height comprised within one standard deviation on either side of the mean and one standard deviation corresponds to the 16th and 84th centiles respectively. Similar figures apply to other measurements (Fig. 3.7).

In the setting up of a centile chart, the characteristic is

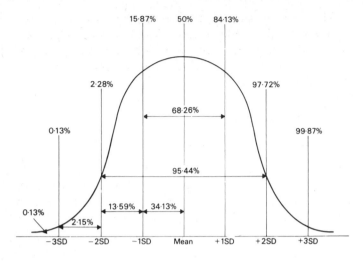

Fig. 3.7 The relationships of centiles to standard deviations in a normally distributed characteristic.

measured in a large number of individuals, either on a one-off basis on many children of different ages (cross-sectional data), or by measuring the same children repeatedly as they grow (longitudinal data). Since longitudinal growth studies take many years to complete, there are a few of them. Most standards include data of both types and are called mixed longitudinal. For each characteristic at each age there will be a value above and below which 50% of children's values lie. This is the 50th centile and means just this, nothing more. If the characteristic is normally distributed, it will also be the mean value but this is not necessarily so (e.g. weight). Centile lines can be drawn for any number because the centile distribution makes no assumption about how the characteristic varies. Conventionally, we have come to draw 3rd, 10th, 25th, 50th, 75th, 90th, and 97th centile lines but there is no special virtue in these numbers (except that for a characteristic which is normally distributed, like height, the 3rd and 97th centiles include 94% of the population and coincide with values plus and minus two standard deviations from the mean).

This description of a characteristic as it is (not necessarily as it should be) is an important concept to grasp in growth assessment. There is no virtue in being near the population mean: the point is readily assimilable in terms of Intelligence Quotient!

Bone age and height prediction

Bone age is a guide to the amount of growth which has already taken place, compared to the amount of growth which is to come. Overall, it plays a part in the general assessment of maturity, but it is a bad guide to the onset of puberty and of little help ever in making a diagnosis. In cases of hypothyroidism, for example, the bone age is generally considerably retarded and in cases of growth hormone deficiency it is moderately retarded, but in neither case is retardation of bone age essential to making the diagnosis and I have patients with both conditions in whom the discovery of a bone age which approached the chronological age delayed investigation, diagnosis and treatment.

There are two main methods of estimating bone age and three systems can be used for the prediction of mature height. The first method uses the *Atlas of Skeletal Development* by Greulich and Pyle (1959). In this method the development of each centre is compared with a series of standard pictures chosen to be typical for boys and girls of different ages. By comparing the radial epiphysis with the standards and noting the age with which it most closely corresponds, followed by the ulnar epiphysis, the first metacarpal epiphysis and so on throughout the bones of the hand and wrist, an average bone age can be calculated. This is laborious but gives accurate and reproducible results. The tables of Bayley and Pinneau (1952), which indicate the proportion of growth which has passed at any one bone age and which have been recently re-published (Post & Richman 1981), can be used to predict mature adult height from a measurement of stature, chronological age, and bone age measured by the Greulich and Pyle

method. The difficulty with the Greulich and Pyle method
is that in clinical practice there is a tendency to compare
the whole X-ray with the whole hand standards. This leads
to a report which is of no help to growth assessment.
Examples of such suspect reports include: 'Bone age
normal for chronological age' — since two standard
deviations of bone age cover approximately 18 months on
either side of chronological age, this does not help very
much. 'The bone age corresponds most closely to the
female standard of 7 years and 10 months' — this does not
help much either, because two standard deviations on
either side of 7 years and 10 months for girls cover 40
months. 'The bone age is between 8 years 10 months and
10 years' — a height prediction for a tall girl aged eight
with a height of 145 cm, based on this would lead to
predictions between 185 cm and 175 cm, which is not
helpful to a decision whether or not treatment is needed to
limit ultimate stature.

The second main method in use is the one described by
Tanner *et al* (1975). In this method each bone is compared
in turn to a series of radiographic standards and a score is
allotted. The scores are added up and compared to
standard scores for age and an exact reading is obtained.
This sounds laborious but in fact takes about 45 seconds if
the scores are added on a pocket calculator. The results can
be used in predictive equations provided in the same text.

The third method of predicting adult height is that of
Roche, Wainer, and Thissen (1975). Here recumbent
length, nude weight, mid-parent stature, and a Greulich
and Pyle bone age are used to predict adult stature. (The
idea of recumbent length and nude weight in an adolescent
clinic conjures up splendid problems for administrators
but adjustments from standing height and weight in
underclothes are permissible!) This method has built in the
problems of estimating bone age by the Atlas method so it
is not a good alternative to the Tanner one on those
grounds.

All these methods when used correctly give reproducible
results but, not surprisingly considering how they were
designed, the newer height prediction tables of Tanner *et al*

and Roche *et al* are superior to those of Bayley and Pinneau for predicting final height in normal subjects. This includes tall normal subjects (Zachmann *et al* 1978), but for subjects with growth disorders and endocrine conditions the older and simpler tables of Bayley and Pinneau give more accurate results, which is not surprising as bone age is the single most important determinant of adult stature when it and chronological age are widely discrepant. For the management of growth disorders both a new and an old system must be to hand.

Pubertal status

This is assessed according to the criteria described by Tanner (1962) and the criteria are as follows:

Boys: genital (penis) development (Fig. 3.8)

Stage 1   Preadolescent: testes, scrotum and penis are of about the same size and proportion as in early childhood.
Stage 2   Enlargement of scrotum and testes. Skin of scrotum reddens and changes in texture. Little or no enlargement of penis at this stage.
Stage 3   Enlargement of penis, which occurs at first mainly in length. Further growth of testes and scrotum.
Stage 4   Increased size of penis with growth in breadth and development of glans. Testes and scrotum larger; scrotal skin darkened.
Stage 5   Genitalia adult in size and shape.

Girls: breast development (Fig. 3.9)

Stage 1   Preadolescent: elevation of papilla only.
Stage 2   Breast bud stage: elevation of breast and papilla as small mound. Enlargement of areolar diameter.
Stage 3   Further enlargement and elevation of breast and areola, with no separation of their contours.
Stage 4   Projection of areola and papilla to form a secondary mound above the level of the breast.
Stage 5   Mature stage: projection of papilla only, due to recession of the areola to the general contour of the breast.

Both sexes: pubic hair (Fig. 3.10)

Stage 1   Preadolescent. The vellus over the pubes is not further developed than that over the abdominal wall, i.e. no pubic hair.

Stage 2   Sparse growth of long, slightly pigmented downy hair, straight or slightly curled, chiefly at the base of the penis or along labia.

Stage 3   Considerably darker, coarser and more curled. The hair spread sparsely over the junction of the pubes.

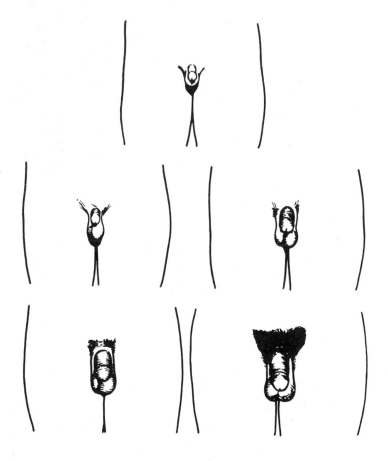

Fig. 3.8   Stages of genital development in boys (1–5).

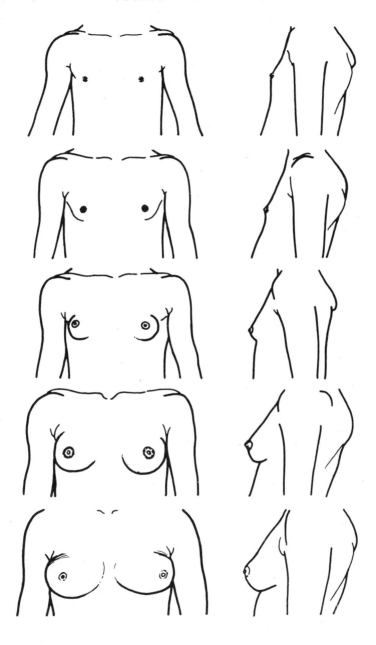

Fig. 3.9 Stages of breast development in girls (1–5).

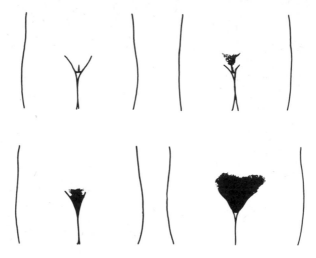

Fig. 3.10   Pubic hair staging (2–5).

Stage 4   Hair now adult in type, but area covered is still considerably smaller than in the adult. No spread to the medial surface of thighs.

Stage 5   Adult in quantity and type with distribution of the horizontal (or classically feminine pattern). Spread to medial surface of thighs but not up linea alba or elsewhere above the base of the inverse triangle (spread up linea alba occurs later and is rated Stage 6)

Both sexes: axillary hair

Stage 1   Preadolescent. No axillary hair.
Stage 2   Scanty growth of slightly pigmented hair.
Stage 3   Hair adult in quality and quantity.

Testicular size should be recorded as testicular volume. This is easily assessed by comparison with standard ovoids and the Prader orchidometer (Fig. 3.11) is an indispensible aid to this purpose. The testis is palpated by one hand and the orchidometer is held in the other. Standards are available against which to compare testicular volume (Zachmann *et al* 1974) and are shown in Fig. 3.12

Fig. 3.11 Prader orchidometer.

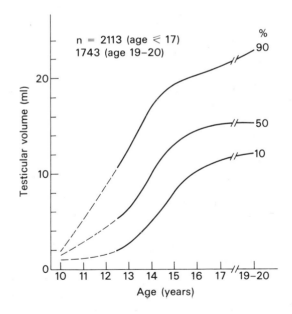

Fig. 3.12 Standards for testicular volume (Zachmann *et al* 1974). Reproduced with permission.

Under no circumstances should these ratings be lumped together in an overall stage of puberty because each depends upon different endocrinological events and each, therefore, has its own significance. A standard rating for a boy might read G (genitalia) 3, PH (pubic hair) 3, Ax (axillary hair) 2, 8/10 (ml for testicular volume in the right and left testes respectively, the figures being written while the examiner looks at the scrotum). For a girl a recording of pubertal stage might be B (breasts) 4, PH (pubic hair) 4, Ax (axillary hair) 2 and then some designation of whether or not menarche has occurred.

GROWTH ASSESSMENT: WHAT TO DO WITH THE MEASUREMENTS

Height is entered on a standard centile chart of the type shown in Fig. 3.13. Here the height of a 13.5 year old boy lies just below the 3rd centile for his chronological age. The 3rd centile means that 3% of boys aged 13.5 have a height less than 141 cm; 50% of children at 13.5 have a height greater than 156 cm and 97% have a height less than 172cm. On the adult side of the chart are entered the centile positions of the heights of the parents (measured if at all possible because the error on reported heights is considerable). In this case, a correction must, of course, be applied to the height of the mother before entering her height directly on a centile chart for boys. This is done by adding 12.6 cm to her height and entering it directly on the boy's chart, 12.6 cm representing the difference in mean heights between adult men and women. In this case, the height of the mother was actually 158 cm and her height has been entered at 170.6 cm (158 + 12.6 cm), which is, of course, on the same (25th) centile as 158 cm is for females on the equivalent female chart. The father's height is entered as measured, at 179 cm. The converse would be done if this were a girl, 12.6 cm being subtracted from the father's height before being entered and the mother's being entered directly. As can be seen from this example, the mid-parental centile coincides approximately with the 50th centile for the population.

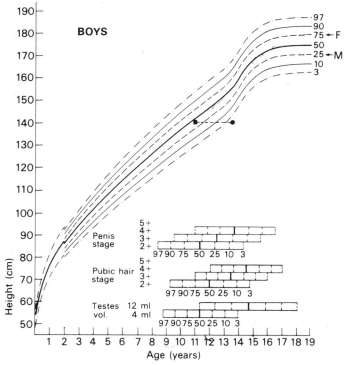

Fig. 3.13 Standard height centile chart.

The third element to be entered on the chart at this stage is the skeletal maturity of the boy. This was estimated to be 11 'years' and is shown on the chart by a solid square joined to the height measurement by a dotted line. This means that 82% of his growth has already passed but as the height for the bone age lies close to the midparental centile, this child has a growth potential which is appropriate for the heights of his parents as long as he continues to grow normally.

In fact, he will probably not quite achieve either his mid-parent centile for height or the centile of his height for bone age because, as can be seen from the bottom of chart, he has not yet shown any signs of entering puberty, no ratings being shown because he is still prepubertal. This means that he is going to have longer than usual prepubertal growth and, as we have already seen, this means that he will be growing increasingly slowly. The later his growth spurt comes, the less it will be and his formal Tanner height prediction works out as follows:

Predicted mature height

= (present height (140.0) × 0.94) − (chronological age (13.5 × 1.9) − (bone age (11.0) × 4.4) + (constant 113)
= 131.6 − 25.6 − 48.4 + 113 = 170.6

The final height nearly always works out on a centile between the height for bone age and height for chronological age and the same is true in reverse for tall statures. I find this helpful in the clinic, although it is not the pukka way of predicting. The other measurements that will have been taken — weight and skinfold thicknesses — can be compared to standard values in exactly the same way.

In practical terms, the gathering of these data has not advanced the diagnosis in any way. To decide whether or not growth is normal a second measurement of height is required. This has to be made after a period of time long enough to allow a difference in height to have occurred which is greater than the error of the measurements of height on each of the two occasions. For practical purposes, this period of time is a minimum of three months under the most ideal measurement conditions, but may be considerably longer if the measurements are not made with great care and accuracy with regard to repeatability.

The difference in height is then divided by the time which has elapsed between the two measurements and a figure is calculated for a rate of growth in terms of centimetres per year. This is difficult to achieve when ordinary calendar months are used and for this reason decimal dates are preferred. This may seem laborious, but greatly facilitates the calculation of growth velocity, which is central to the making of a diagnosis.

A table of the calendar on the decimal system is shown

in Table 3.1 and decimal age is calculated by subtracting the decimal date of birth from the decimal date of observation. If a boy was born on 2nd June 1977 (77.416) and today's date is 3rd November 1982 (82.838), his decimal age is 5.422 years. If we measure him again on 23rd April 1983 (83.307), 0.469 of a year will have elapsed. If he has grown 2.8 cm in that time, his rate of growth is 2.8 divided by 0.469 = 6.0 cm per year. This is then entered or reference can be made to the standard chart shown in Fig. 3.14 at the age half-way between the measurement dates, at 5.6 years.

Great confusion is caused by velocity centiles. The centiles exist because not every child grows at exactly the

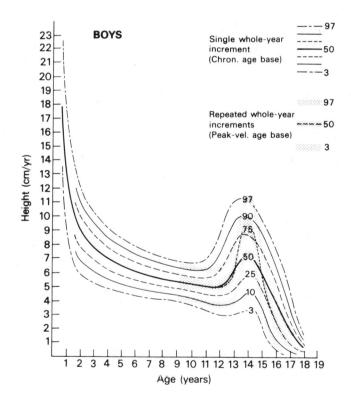

Fig. 3.14 Height velocity chart.

Table 3.1 Decimals of a year.

	1 Jan	2 Feb	3 Mar	4 Apr	5 May	6 Jun	7 Jul	8 Aug	9 Sep	10 Oct	11 Nov	12 Dec
1	000	085	162	247	329	414	496	581	666	748	833	915
2	003	088	164	249	332	416	499	584	668	751	836	918
3	005	090	167	252	334	419	501	586	671	753	838	921
4	008	093	170	255	337	422	504	589	674	756	841	923
5	011	096	173	258	340	425	507	592	677	759	844	926
6	014	099	175	260	342	427	510	595	679	762	847	929
7	016	101	178	263	345	430	512	597	682	764	849	932
8	019	104	181	266	348	433	515	600	685	767	852	934
9	022	107	184	268	351	436	518	603	688	770	855	937
10	025	110	186	271	353	438	521	605	690	773	858	940
11	027	112	189	274	356	441	523	608	693	775	860	942
12	030	115	192	277	359	444	526	611	696	778	863	945
13	033	118	195	279	362	447	529	614	699	781	866	948
14	036	121	197	282	364	449	532	616	701	784	868	951
15	038	123	200	285	367	452	534	619	704	786	871	953

16	041	126	203	288	370	455	537	622	707	789	874	956
17	044	129	205	290	373	458	540	625	710	792	877	959
18	047	132	208	293	375	460	542	627	712	795	879	962
19	049	134	211	296	378	463	545	630	715	797	882	964
20	052	137	214	299	381	466	548	633	718	800	885	967
21	055	140	216	301	384	468	551	636	721	803	888	970
22	058	142	219	304	386	471	553	638	723	805	890	973
23	060	145	222	307	389	474	556	641	726	808	893	975
24	063	148	225	310	392	477	559	644	729	811	896	978
25	066	151	227	312	395	479	562	647	731	814	899	981
26	068	153	230	315	397	482	564	649	734	816	901	984
27	071	156	233	318	400	485	567	652	737	819	904	986
28	074	159	236	321	403	488	570	655	740	822	907	989
29	077		238	323	405	490	573	658	742	825	910	992
30	079		241	326	408	493	575	660	745	827	912	995
31	082		244		411		578	663		830		997

same speed year by year. Taken overall, it is necessary for the growth velocity of an individual child to mean on the 50th centile if he is not to lose or gain in respect of his peers. Growth in height, which has to take place over a given period of time is, perhaps, like a motor journey of 300 miles (480 km). If this is to be achieved in six hours the average speed must be 50 mph (80 kph). This speed is easily practicable on the major highway, but not possible in the country lane. The driving speed on one has to cancel out

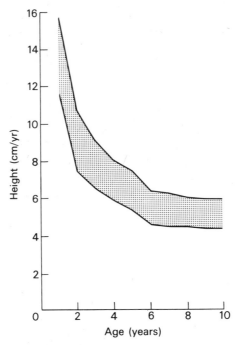

Fig. 3.15 Height velocity chart showing acceptable limits for boys and girls. For use in school clinics.

HOW TO USE THIS CHART

1 Measure height on two occasions.
2 Plot the rate of growth (cm/year) against the age of the child midway between the two measurements, e.g. Heights measured at ages 4 and 6 show a difference of 12 cm. Rate is 6 cm/year which should be plotted at age 5.
3 Seek advice for rates falling outside the hatched area.

that on the other if the object is to be achieved. So it is with growth and, as will be seen later, is of crucial importance.

Strictly to compare our example with the centiles we need to follow him for a whole year, but obviously the chances of his being abnormal are pretty remote if he is so near the 50th centile over six months. It should be noted here that calculation of velocity in this way is quite independent of height already achieved or of any other measure but should possibly be related to the former. So-called conditional standards of height velocity based on the actual height at a given age and the growth which might be expected in the next year do exist (Cameron 1980) and are currently under clinical trial. For practical purposes the purist approach, which conditional standards exemplify, is not necessary, the child's growth velocity being either manifestly abnormal or probably, as here, within normal limits. For simplicity I have prepared a chart for use in local school clinics which is shown in Fig. 3.15.

With estimates of height, parental heights, skeletal maturity, height velocity and nutritional status, growth assessment is complete and we are in a position to consider the problems which confront doctors in the diagnosis and management of children with growth disorders.

REFERENCES

BAYLEY N. & PINNEAU S.R. (1952) Table for predicting adult height from skeletal age revised for use with the Greulich-Pyle hand standards. *Journal of Pediatrics* **40**, 423-441. (Erratum **41**, 371.)

BUCKLER J.M.H. (1979) *A Reference Manual of Growth and Development.* Blackwell Scientific Publications, Oxford.

CAMERON N. (1980) Conditional standards for growth in height of British children from 5.0 to 15.99 years of age. *Annals of Human Biology* **7**, 331-7.

GREULICH W.W. & PYLE S.I. (1959) *Radiographic Atlas of Skeletal Development of Hand and Wrist.* Stanford University Press, California.

POST E.M. & RICHMAN R.A. (1981) A condensed table for predicting adult stature. *Journal of Pediatrics* **98**, 440-442.

ROCHE A.F., WAINER H. & THISSEN D. (1975) The RWT method for the prediction of adult stature. *Pediatrics* **56**, 1027-33.

TANNER J.M. (1962) *Growth at Adolescence,* 2nd edn. Blackwell Scientific Publications, Oxford

TANNER J.M., WHITEHOUSE R.H., MARSHALL W.A. *et al* (1975) *Assessment of skeletal maturation and prediction of adult height.* Academic Press, New York.

WHITELAW A.G.L. (1976) Influence of maternal obesity on subcutaneous fat in the newborn. *British Medical Journal* **1**, 985-6.

ZACHMANN M., PRADER A., KIND H.P., *et al* (1974) Testicular volume during adolescence. *Helvetica Paediatrica Acta* **29**, 61-72.

ZACHMANN M., SOBRADILLO B., FRANK M. *et al* (1978) Bayley-Pinneau, Roache-Wainer-Thissen, and Tanner height predictions in normal children and in patients with various pathologic conditions. *Journal of Pediatrics* **93**, 749-55.

CHAPTER 4

The Small Child

Summary of diagnosis and therapy-orientated management of short stature

1 Measure child's height and an index of nutritional status (skinfold thickness or weight).
2 Measure parental heights.
3 Plot centile positions on a standard chart. Is the child short for his parents?
4 Has he normal body proportions? If not, he needs a skeletal survey for disproportionate short stature.
5 Does he look normal? If not, has he dysmorphic features to make a diagnosis? (Smith 1976)
6 If he has proportionate short stature and looks normal, measure growth velocity. If low, investigate and treat accordingly.
7 If growth velocity is normal, measure skeletal maturity to assess growth prognosis and ensure that velocity continues to be normal.

THE CLINICAL APPROACH (Fig. 4.1)

Small children fall into three groups, those who are small and normal, those who are small as a result of an earlier event or congenital anomaly which cannot now be corrected, and those whose short stature is due to a remedial condition. It is obviously to the latter that our attention must be particularly directed.

The categorisation of an individual child depends upon growth assessment and clinical examination. It does not depend, at least in the first instance, on laboratory investigation which should not be employed until

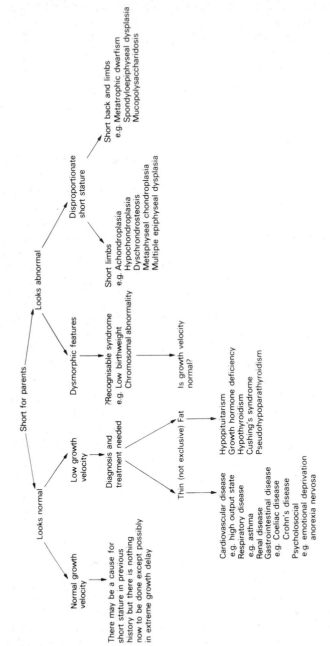

Fig. 4.1   The differential diagnosis of short stature.

auxological data indicate it to be necessary. Many children are investigated for 'failure to thrive' because they are small but many are actually growing normally at the time of investigation. In such instances the results of the investigations often need investigating, because they are so coarse a measurement of normality. Only when a child is actually *failing* to thrive will investigation help.

The necessary measurements at a first visit to a clinic are height and parental heights together with an assessment of nutritional status. Reliance has often to be placed on the reported height of one parent and this tends to bias the data collection, since every man likes to regard his wife as smaller than he. Consequently males underestimate the heights of their wives; females are unpredictable in this respect, but mother–father correlations of reported height are spuriously high. Heights should be measured and where this cannot be done, comparison with the height of a member of staff ('How does your wife's height compare with that of this nurse/receptionist?') is probably the next best tactic. The height of the child is entered on the standard chart and those of the parents on the relevant centiles (p.45). Is the child within the parental centiles? Distribution of height in the population is reduced in the children of given parents by the parent–child correlation of height, which reflects the genetic contribution to its determination. In effect, the standard deviation of height is reduced by one-third so that the mid-parental centile ± 8.5 cm (2 s.d.) gives the range of centiles one might expect in 95% of the children of given parents. Charts are available which take this fact into account (Tanner *et al* 1970) but puberty complicates the statistics and so they are only used for children from ages 2 to 9 years. The mid-parental centile and target height calculated as above is more than adequate in clinical practice.

If a child's height is within the limits for parental height, the chances of there being anything wrong are remote, always assuming that the parents themselves are normal. This last caveat has considerable practical importance. Most skeletal disorders arise as new mutations but they are also inherited as dominant characteristics. Some endocrine disorders are also inherited (in various ways) and what was untreatable in the parents may well be susceptible to treatment in their children. Nor may a parent's height be the full expression of his genetic potential if he or she was reared in adverse environmental circumstances. Caution should be exercised in comparing the child with parents whose own stature is conspicuously short. If a child does seem to be short for his parents, has he a congenital abnormality or a treatable condition? Here clinical examination may help and further anthropometric measurements may make things easier. The measurement of skinfold thickness (p.33) will provide an objective estimate of nutritional status and charts are available with which to make comparison (Fig. 4.2).

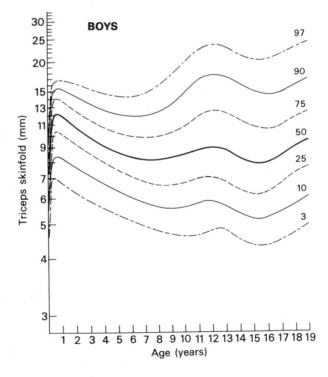

Fig. 4.2 Standards centile chart of triceps skinfold thickness in boys (Tanner & Whitehouse 1975).

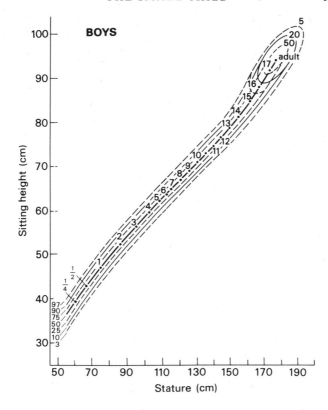

Fig. 4.3 Sitting height for stature chart.

The measurement of sitting height (Fig. 3.3, p.31) helps to define body proportions. The use of sitting height for stature charts has been only moderately helpful in practice (Fig. 4.3) and comparison of sitting height centile position with centile position for leg length seems to define disproportion more accurately. The chart which is used for this purpose is illustrated in Fig. 4.4. Sitting height is compared directly for age; subischial leg length represents stature less sitting height. On the chart, provision has been made to plot the difference between their standard deviation scores to test whether body proportions are within the limits of normal (Tanner 1978). The calculation of standard deviation scores requires access to means and

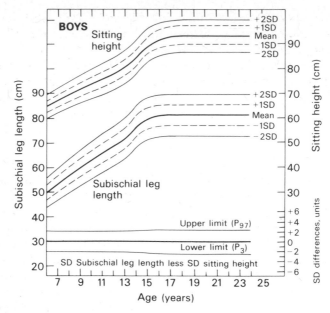

Fig. 4.4 Sitting height and subischial leg length chart.

standard deviations in the normal population, but the charts for sitting height and leg length are plotted as standard deviations rather than centiles to make this easier (see Fig. 4.4). The plotting of sitting height and leg length is not difficult and gives a good idea of which body segment is short.

The association of a number of dysmorphic features to comprise an eponymous syndrome is a satisfying intellectual exercise but not of much practical help. Nevertheless, it is true that parents often find it comforting to know that other children are affected similarly to their own child. There are several useful compendia of syndromes (Bergsma 1979; Smith 1976) and many other descriptions of individual syndromes. Computers have now been programmed to match clinical observations with existing data on different syndromes and the making of a diagnosis certainly does help in predicting the future and in genetic counselling. On the other hand, not all children with a syndrome have or will acquire all the features and the allocation of a 'funny-looking kid' (FLK) label may effectively prevent further thought directed towards a diagnosis in an individual instance. Finally, because possession of a syndrome does not exclude a continuing growth problem and because a number of the syndromes are associated with endocrinological abnormalities of one sort or another (Aarskog 1981), the principles of growth assessment should apply equally to children with dysmorphic syndromes as to any other short child.

The diagnosis and correction of treatable conditions is much more rewarding. Treatment means correcting an abnormal growth velocity. Diagnosis, therefore, means recognising such a velocity. It is obvious that instantaneous treatment is not available for growth. Nor can the clock be put back, so treatment is prospective and aimed at maximising growth potential *at the time of diagnosis.* As already indicated, the assessment of skeletal maturity will measure the proportion of growth which has taken place. This is history and cannot be altered. What treatment seeks is to allow the remaining proportion to be realised. Lack of treatment will mean that this will not be realised. Consequently, the earlier a poor growth velocity is recognised and treated, the better the ultimate outcome will be.

The assessment of skeletal maturity is not a diagnostic tool but the measurement of growth velocity is, and in a child growing slowly there is a diagnosis to be made and a therapy to be employed. Rational therapy may or may not be successful, depending upon whether the reasoning behind it was correct. Empirical therapy is what is needed. Fortunately, in the growth field, we have less of a problem than in much of medical practice, since rationality and empiricism coincide more frequently.

PROPORTIONATE SHORT STATURE

Syndromes

In most cases, children with a syndrome who are short, may have been of low birthweight and may also not be as well endowed intellectually as the rest of the family. The dysmorphic physical features dictate the syndrome. Since there are many syndromes and since many children do not fit exactly the description of a syndrome, categorisation of an individual patient is relatively unimportant compared to establishing whether he is growing normally.

If he is not, the principles of investigation and treatment apply as Figs. 4.5 and 4.6 indicate. Here, children with Bloom syndrome (low birthweight, a light-sensitive rash and chromosomal aberrations) and Poland's anomaly (short stature and absence of pectoralis major with or

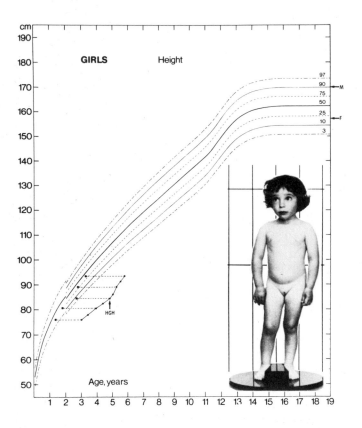

Fig. 4.5 Bloom syndrome and the response to growth hormone treatment.

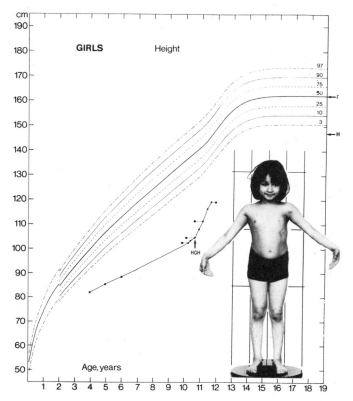

Fig. 4.6 Poland anomaly and the response to growth hormone treatment.

without cutaneous syndactyly) were found to be growing excessively slowly. They were investigated and found to have at least partial deficiency of growth hormone. Administration of growth hormone resulted in a good response. Not all children with these particular syndromes are responsive to growth hormone but the point is that, even within the confines of a recognisable syndrome, it is worth taking up the cause of a very low growth velocity, since nothing can be done for a child with a syndrome and a normal growth velocity.

Two syndromes deserve special mention. The first is the association of low birthweight and its resultant short stature, to which reference has already been made (page

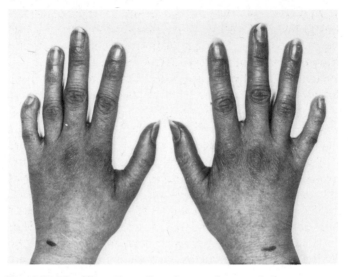

Fig. 4.7 The Silver–Russell syndrome: characteristic appearance of the hands.

19). Whether there are dysmorphic characteristics or not (Russell 1954; Silver 1964; Tanner *et al* 1975) is unimportant, but birth histories are most important. Birth length is so seldom known in the United Kingdom that it is hardly worth asking the question. Elsewhere it may hopefully be otherwise. Birthweight is compared to standard centiles in the normal way, allowance being made for maternal height (Tanner & Thomson 1970). It is important to enquire the birthweights of other family members; sometimes within-family low birthweight provides striking help. The highly characteristic and almost essential history for the diagnosis of short stature due to low birthweight is the formidable difficulty of feeding such children in infancy. So invariable is the response of the mother that the diagnosis is in serious doubt if she does not strongly echo questions about this aspect of her child's behaviour. Sometimes, indeed, it is permissable to make a diagnosis of the Silver-Russell syndrome on the basis of clinical features (characteristic facies (Fig. 7.3, p.116), body asymmetry, thinness and clinodactyly (incurving and shortening) of the fifth fingers

— Fig. 4.7) and the feeding history in the absence of grossly low birthweight. I take these children to be at the upper end of the birthweight distribution for the syndrome (Tanner *et al* 1975). The postnatal growth of these children is characteristically normal; consequently, nothing can be done to improve it — nor can they be made to eat.

The second syndrome is that of Turner (1938), which was subsequently shown to be the result of an absence of one X chromosome. Mosaicism is common but the effect of Turner syndrome on growth is to add persistent low growth velocity to a prenatal growth deficit (Brook *et al* 1974). In patients with Turner syndrome who have ceased growing, the same relationship of their height with that of their parents is maintained as in the normal population. This means that tall parents may not recognise the syndrome in their children early on whereas, for short parents, it is extremely difficult to predict a satisfactory growth outcome.

Turner syndrome is common and there may not necessarily be the well known dysmorphic features — an increased carrying angle, widely spaced nipples, neck webbing and so on. The most invariable feature is short stature but the main implication of the diagnosis is, of course, on pubertal development and reproductive capacity. Sometimes, as in Fig. 4.8, an extremely low growth velocity (low even for patients with Turner syndrome) may deserve investigation. In the case illustrated, investigation showed the patient to lack growth hormone; therapy restored Turner-like growth and will result in a final height which will not be quite so socially disadvantageous as it might have been. Again, a low growth velocity was the key to investigation and treatment, since growth hormone has been shown not to be effective in promoting the growth of most girls with this condition (Tanner *et al* 1971).

The association of Turner syndrome with endocrine disorders, especially autoimmune ones, is well recognised. The demonstration of antibodies to growth hormone-producing cells of the pituitary in one very short patient with Turner syndrome, offered a fascinating insight into a possible mechanism but they could not be found in the patient in Fig. 4.8 (G.F. Bottazzo, personal communication).

Clear evidence is emerging that anabolic steroids are useful in promoting growth velocity without excessive bone age advancement in patients with Turner syndrome (Urban *et al* 1979). Although the results of trials still in progress are not fully available, there seems little doubt that the administration of oxandrolone in small amounts before oestrogens are introduced will maintain an adequate growth velocity for longer than occurs naturally in the Turner syndrome. My current practice is to

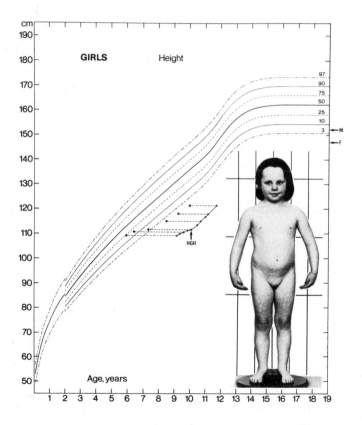

Fig. 4.8   Turner syndrome and growth hormone deficiency.

introduce a small dose of anabolic steroid at the age of ten years or when growth velocity has fallen to less than 4 cm per year, whichever is the sooner. The dose employed is small (< 0.1 mg/kg /24 hr) and such treatment maintains growth velocity at around 5 cm per year without excessively advancing bone age. At the age of twelve years, oestrogens are added. There is no virtue in delaying the institution of oestrogen therapy beyond this age because the diminishing growth velocity which precedes pubertal development progressively lowers the height from which the pubertal growth can begin. Secondly, delay further separates the girl with the Turner syndrome from the pubertal development of her peers.

The introduction of oestrogen should be done very gradually. This is important first because the introduction of large doses of oestrogen produces unsatisfactory breast development with deeply pigmented and crusted nipples, whereas the gradual introduction of treatment produces a much better cosmetic result. Secondly, large doses of oestrogen reduce somatomedin generation and reduce growth velocity. Current practice is to introduce not more than 10 μg of ethinyloestradiol daily. This should be continued for approximately six months or until breakthrough bleeding occurs, whichever is the sooner. If breakthrough bleeding does occur, norethisterone acetate 5 mg daily should be provided for five days and all treatment then stopped for a week, which will produce a normal period. After this or after six months of continuous oestrogen without breakthrough bleeding, an intermittent oestrogen regimen should be started. It will be necessary to provide a progestogen as well and a very satisfactory combination is provided in an ultra-low dose oral contraceptive pill which contains 20 μg of ethinyloestradiol (e.g. Loestrin 20). This treatment will be employed for about six months and final breast development can be produced by increasing the dose of ethinyloestradiol to 30 μg daily, again in an oral contraceptive preparation containing both oestrogen and a progestogen. In the majority of cases this sequential approach produces very satisfactory breast development and probably maximises growth potential. It is almost never necessary to exceed 30μg of ethinyloestradiol daily. To do so rarely increases breast size. Occasionally, in instances where breast development is still not satisfactory, it may be desirable to proceed to augmentation mammoplasty, since there is no further mileage to be gained from endocrinological manipulation.

The induction of puberty in these patients takes therefore, not less than two years, a time which corresponds reasonably to the time for the development of natural puberty. Thus it probably offers the best prospect for maximising growth and for ensuring normal physical and psychological maturation of the patient during pubertal development.

Small/delay

The largest group of children that doctors see are small and normal. They are the 3% of normal children below the 3rd centile line and in no way does their centile position deserve investigation *per se*. The hallmark of their growth is its normal velocity. If that is established, investigation is pointless and unnecessary. The results of tests must be normal in normal people and when they are reported as abnormal it is the tests that are suspect, not the children.

Whether or not growth delay also exists is irrelevant to making a diagnosis, but helpful to ultimate stature. Growth delay, which is measured by retardation of bone age, is the reason why the child of parents of average size may be small for them and so draw attention to themselves. As a group, children who manifest short stature and a significant degree of growth delay go relatively late into puberty. Since the discrepancy in height and physical maturity between the patient and his peers then becomes conspicuous I find it prudent to warn of this in advance. Fig. 4.9 illustrates the point.

Ben is the son of tall parents. He has mild to moderately severe asthma which is easily controlled by disodium cromoglycate. His case exhibits all the features of growth delay and, when he was twelve, I warned him and his

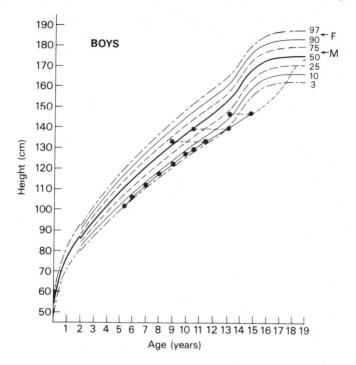

Fig. 4.9 Normal velocity growth within the centiles may fall below the centiles at time of puberty if growth delay is also present.

parents of how prepubertal deceleration would affect him by drawing on the chart the curve that I predicted for his growth. The reassurance that I was able to offer when I saw him at ages 13 and 15 by demonstrating that he was precisely the heights I had predicted was worth many hours of psychotherapy.

A second case of asthma is worth mentioning here. Christopher was referred to me at age 16 because his growth 'seemed to be falling off'. He had had severe asthma throughout his childhood, so severe that he had had to receive corticosteroid therapy. On the chart (Fig. 4.10) I have plotted his growth in height for chronological age. I have also plotted height for skeletal maturity based on the estimates of bone age which I made from the radiographs which were sent to me and, parenthetically, the reports that the clinician was receiving from his radiologist on the same radiographs. These demonstrate why the clinician suddenly became alarmed when the bone age 'seemed to have suddenly advanced so rapidly'. It had not done so, of course: the previous reports had been wrong. This boy's case is an illustrative one. The first point to be made is that it is better to be alive and short than tall and dead: recourse to steroid therapy is necessary on some occasions and this valuable therapy should not be denied sick children. The consequences of diminishing growth velocity on the one hand but not proportionately arresting skeletal maturation on the other have, however, to be faced. In such a situation, reduction in growth prognosis is

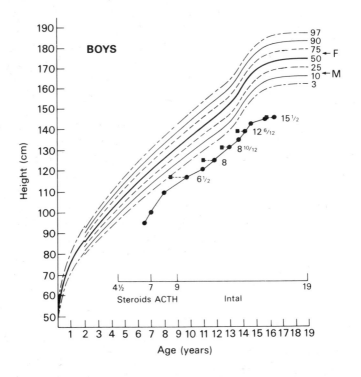

Fig. 4.10   The consequence of steroids and ACTH treatment on growth and bone age.

inevitable and irreversible. In this case the final height was predictable from the chart at age 18 and possibly would have been predictable earlier if radiographs had been available.

The second point is to explore the hypothesis that it is less dangerous from a growth point of view to use ACTH than steroids. I have never understood the logic of this suggestion and am not satisfied that it has ever been properly tested from the point of view of growth analysis. Growth velocity at the time of treatment has certainly been shown to be better on ACTH than on steroids (Friedman & Strang 1966) and the present case illustrates this point. I think it is probable that adrenal androgens are stimulated by ACTH (*pace* congenital adrenal hyperplasia) in addition to cortisol which is the therapeutic agent. Thus, using ACTH is equivalent to treating with glucocorticoids and anabolic steroids together. The effect of such combined treatment on bone age would be considerable and the ultimate stature of children treated with ACTH may well not be better than that of children treated with steroids, even if things looked better in the short term. This theory needs testing empirically.

Parenthetically, it is worth mentioning one of the other major indications for the use of steroids in paediatric practice, Still's disease. Here the complications of steroid use are compounded by the fact that bone age advances in any joint affected by hyperaemia contingent on inflammation. This is most characteristically seen in the arthritides but can also affect growth in children with connective tissue disorders and even locally with tenosynovitis (Barbara Ansell, personal communication). There are thus two processes at work in children with connective tissue disorders treated with steroids which lead to short stature.

Low growth velocity

A low growth velocity, regardless of absolute height, requires investigation. There has to be an explanation, although whether or not it is remedial depends, of course, on the nature of that explanation. In the majority of instances the origin of short stature (perhaps shortening stature is a more appropriate description) lies in the complexity of socioeconomic deprivation (Lacey & Parkin 1974, Vimpani *et al* 1977). The reversible hypopituitarism of the emotionally deprived child was first recognised by Powell *et al* (1967) and has been documented many times by others. The reversibility is rapid: investigation after even one overnight stay out of the disadvantaged environment may miss the blunted growth hormone responsiveness to the usual tests. The beauty of the work of Vimpani *et al* (1977) was that it was all done with a mobile clinic in the field.

Children with eating disorders but without classical anorexia nervosa present not infrequently with short stature and are found to have a poor growth velocity. The treatment of such patients (and indeed the problem of socioeconomic deprivation causing short stature) is very much more difficult than treatment of orthodox organic disease. At present, because the social class distribution of patients attending growth disorder clinics is not representative of the distribution in the population and because the problem does not present to doctors as often as it exists, clinicians are only seeing the tip of the iceberg. There is undoubtedly a mass of poorly grown and poorly growing people for whom the answers are more political than medical.

Low growth velocity may be a manifestation of any disease. Most diseases in childhood are short-lived and growth is moderately robust, even in those that are not. Thus asthma has to be quite severe before it affects growth velocity, although that it does so is not in doubt. The characteristic cough at night and on exercise is frequently overlooked as a sign of undertreated asthma. Low growth velocity which is associated with respiratory, cardiovascular, renal or gastrointestinal disease is generally associated with a poor nutritional status. Skinfold thicknesses, therefore, are very helpful in pointing a diagnosis but all sorts of medical conditions declare themselves in a growth clinic.

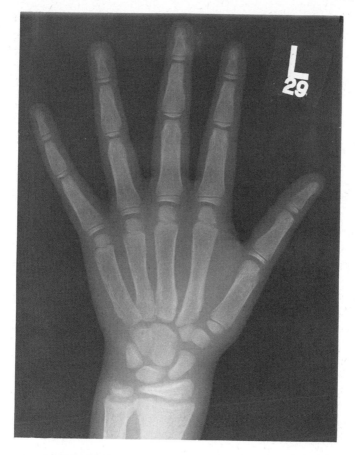

Fig. 4.11 Rachitic changes in a child referred for short stature who had phosphate-losing rickets.

Therese (Fig. 4.11), for example, was referred for evaluation of short stature. It was only by noticing the rachitic changes in the hand X-ray taken for the estimation of skeletal maturity that her phosphate-losing rickets was diagnosed.

Julian (Fig. 4.12), on the other hand, represents the classical problem of occult coeliac disease. His short stature and thinness called for a diagnosis of gastrointestinal pathology, regardless of the fact that his

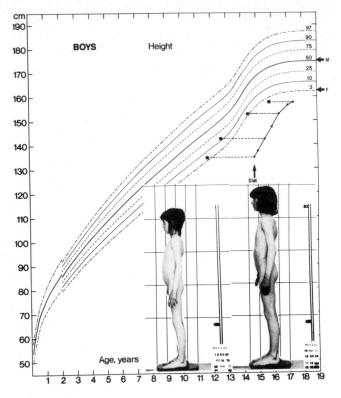

Fig. 4.12 Occult coeliac disease.

growth hormone responsiveness to hypoglycaemia was
blunted. This is well documented in coeliac disease
(Vanderscheuren-Lodeweyckx *et al* 1973) and so is
abnormality in secretion of other pituitary hormones
(Vanderscheuren-Lodeweyckx *et al* 1977).

Inflammatory bowel disease is another catch situation,
which may draw attention to itself by aches and pains in
addition to diarrhoea. Here growth hormone responses
tend to be exaggerated rather than impaired (Tenore *et al*
1977) and somatomedin deficiency may be the cause of the
low growth velocity in this situation, as it seems to be in
malnutrition (Grant *et al* 1973). In that situation, re-
feeding lowers growth hormone levels (Pimstone *et al*

1968) and causes a rise in levels of somatomedin (Almqrist & Rune 1961). Certainly it pays to wear what Dr M. H. Pappworth — teacher to generations of candidates for Membership of the Royal College of Physicians of London — used to call 'wide-angled lenses' in planning the investigation of a low growth velocity.

Endocrine disorder is therapeutically the most rewarding diagnosis to make. Endocrine problems should be sought in all children who are growing slowly without other explanation. This is irrespective of other diagnosis or syndrome but usually such children are well nourished and well in themselves. Investigation demands measurement of all the pituitary hormones in the basal state and after appropriate stimulation (Brook 1978) as well as measurement of thyroxine levels. It is prudent to measure the haemoglobin and levels of calcium, phosphorus, alkaline phosphatase, urea and creatinine at the same time. An initial screen also includes radiography of the skull and assessment of visual fields. This investigation of short stature takes four hours and the answer given will usually be complete, although, of course, occasionally other lines of investigation are revealed which require a further series of tests. An enlarged pituitary fossa is an example of such a situation.

Iatrogenic short stature

The problems of using steroids have already been discussed but there is a further cause of growth deficiency now becoming obvious, that associated with radiotherapeutic treatment of leukaemia and cerebral tumours. Although any space-occupying lesion in childhood may result in short stature due to endocrine dysfunction, problems of puberty are a more common endocrine presentation (see below). Much more important, however, are the pressure effects resulting in symptoms of headache and vomiting and signs of papilloedema and visual field defect. Craniopharyngioma, in particular, accounts for 10% of all cerebral tumours in childhood and cerebral tumours comprise 12% of childhood neoplastic disease.

Regrettably, by the time the majority of children come to treatment for what is potentially a curable condition, irreparable visual defect has occurred.

Following neurosurgical intervention and/or the exposure of the hypothalamo–pituitary axis to radiotherapy, a number of endocrinological dysfunctions can result. In the case of surgery, diabetes insipidus is frequent and its management does not form part of this text. Gonadotrophin deficiency is almost invariable following neurosurgical treatment of craniopharyngioma and ACTH deficiency, growth hormone deficiency and TSH deficiency also occur in association. Replacement of all these hormones may become necessary over a period of time but, certainly as far as growth hormone is concerned, the need for treatment should be based on auxological considerations rather than on endocrinological profiles, since normal or even accelerated growth over a variable period of time, is certainly well documented in a patient with biochemical growth hormone deficiency following treatment.

Treatment

Once a diagnosis of a low growth velocity has been made, treatment follows. It may be in the form of a diet, of treatment of an underlying condition, or as hormone replacement. In all cases an increment in growth velocity is the reward and catch-up is what is sought.

The concept of catch-up, first described by Prader *et al* (1963), is important. In true catch-up, the velocity increases to such an extent that the original growth curve is attained and thereafter growth proceeds normally. Catch-up with delay means that growth is restored to normal in the end (Tanner 1978). Whether it reaches its genetically predictable target depends upon how soon growth deficit is spotted and to what extent skeletal maturation has been retarded whilst growth velocity has been diminished. The clinician starts treatment with a given height, bone age and height prognosis and it is the last he aims to achieve. Because a child cannot grow without advancing bone age, the doctor treating short stature cannot improve the prognosis he finds. The results are better, therefore, the quicker and younger he starts treatment so that as little height prognosis as possible has been lost.

Which catch-up process occurs probably has to do both with age and with the duration and severity of the disease process. Fig. 4.13 shows the growth curves of two patients in my clinic, Louise and Thomas, both of whom have idiopathic isolated growth hormone deficiency. Louise was more severely affected than Thomas in that she was shorter earlier and her response to treatment has been more spectacular. I thought Thomas had simple growth delay when I first met him and was surprised by his low growth velocity. His partial deficiency of growth hormone secretion showed a good response to treatment but, even in

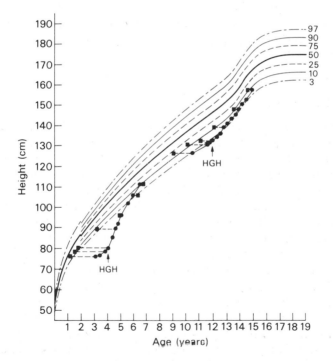

Fig. 4.13 Growth in idiopathic isolated growth hormone deficiency.

a more severely affected case aged more than twelve years, it is rare to get catch-up growth as good as in other disorders (e.g. coeliac disease (Fig. 4.12)). On the whole it is also true that response to growth hormone is less in children whose growth hormone deficiency is the result of organic disease (cerebral tumours, etc.), including those whose growth hormone deficiency follows cranial irradiation (Shalet & Beardwell 1979).

The use of growth hormone requires discussion. In true idiopathic isolated growth hormone deficiency, its use and effectiveness are well known and well documented (Tanner 1972). To a degree, response to treatment is dose-related (Frasier *et al* 1977; Preece *et al* 1976) and an interesting exercise is to compare frequency of administration and dose of growth hormone administered. Review of the experience of the Medical Research Council trial of human growth hormone in the United Kingdom and reports in the literature from other users of growth hormone, mostly in the United States but also in Switzerland and Norway, indicates that a cost- effective regimen uses about 700 units of growth hormone per annum per child administered three times weekly (Preece 1981).

By 'cost-effective' is meant a regimen which achieves good acceleration of growth velocity and a reasonable amount of growth in terms of millimetres of growth achieved/units GH/year. Using 30 units of growth hormone per week produces splendid acceleration (8.4 cm per year) but 15 units produces 8.0 cm per year and 9 units 7.7 cm per year. The high-dose regimen achieves overall only 0.05 mm of growth/unit of GH used/year, the medium 0.1, and lower 0.2 mm/unit/year. Such figures are highly pertinent to the supply of growth hormone.

The questions to which we do not have answers are what constitutes partial growth hormone deficiency, whether the spectrum of partial growth hormone deficiency runs into the diagnostic category of small/delay, whether growth hormone would be effective in small normal children and if it was whether it should be used. In this context the claim by Rudman *et al* (1981) that there are normal short children whose own growth hormone is ineffective but who respond to exogenous supplies has caused much concern, not least to those who safeguard supplies of material used for treatment. There are a number of odd aspects to this study (why children growing so slowly are called 'normal' being the most pertinent) which must be regarded as *sub judice* at present. In the future, if growth hormone supplies become plentiful as a result of genetic engineering, these queries will be answered.

Partial growth hormone deficiency definitely exists as a clinical entity (Tanner *et al* 1971) and exogenous augmentation of endogenous growth hormone secretion results in catch-up growth. Administration of growth hormone has not properly been tested in truly normal subjects; nor, probably, can it be so tested because of the risk of inducing the formation of growth hormone antibodies in otherwise normal children. Fortunately, the formation of growth-inhibiting antibodies to growth hormone is not a common occurrence, but it does happen and there seems to be no solution to the problem when it does. Accordingly, giving growth hormone to children growing normally is a bad idea. Theoretically if one could give enough growth hormone, normal children should get bigger with treatment (pituitary giants would otherwise not exist) but there is unlikely to be material available or money to buy it if it were to test this possibility in the near future.

In the United Kingdom, however, we have reached the stage of finding that our main difficulty is to separate partial growth hormone deficiency from delayed growth, especially when the prepubertal deceleration of the child with small/delay makes him grow exceedingly slowly — and may be associated with poor growth hormone responsiveness to the normal stimuli. At present we approach this clinical problem more by intuition than by science and have fortunately hitherto had sufficient material to afford to be generous in doubtful cases.

Treatment, then, is aimed at increasing growth velocity and is used when growth velocity is low. Replacement should be physiological and exhibition of supra-physiological doses of hormones is not productive. This applies conspicuously to the case of hypothyroidism, when the administration of excessive doses of thyroxin leads to a disproportionate advance in skeletal maturation without such a marked increase in growth velocity. The replacement dose of thyroxin is 0.1 mg/m²/day (Abbasi & Aldige 1977, Rezvani & DeGeorge 1977) and doses administered significantly in excess of this level advance skeletal maturation at a rate greater than they promote growth in height. The consequence is a loss of growth potential which may not be very important if the bone age is greatly retarded, but which may be disastrous if it is not. Great care must be exercised in the administration of any effective drug and it is certainly true in this context that no drug is effective without carrying a danger of inducing undesirable side effects. This applies particularly to the use of steroid hormones to assist delayed growth. In patients who are going late into puberty and whose prepubertal deceleration can be so extreme as almost to come to a standstill before being followed by a normal pubertal growth spurt (Fig. 4.14), the psychological consequences may be very severe. Since this is the time when

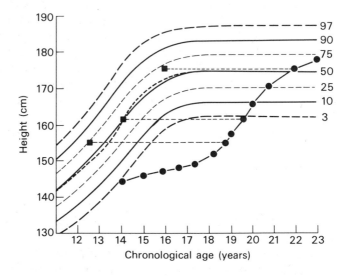

Fig. 4.14 Extreme growth delay.

performance at school is at a premium, such problems can have devastating long-term consequences. Accordingly it is necessary to consider whether anything can be done to help the situation.

In the ordinary course of events the pubertal growth spurt occurs in boys when their testes reach 12-15 ml. It occurs in girls as breast development occurs. In girls, therefore, the first signs of puberty will solve the problem, whereas in boys it may be between one and three years after the first signs of puberty that the growth spurt occurs. In situations of extreme delay, it is necessary to consider whether sexual development or height is the major cause of the problem, since the treatment is different. For the former, treatment with gonadotrophins and/or sex hormones is required (see Chapter 10). For the latter, the use of anabolic steroids or of sex steroids can be extremely effective. Two points need to be made: the first is that treatment can be relatively very short and yet induce the onset of a growth spurt. Secondly, very small doses may be effective. At the time of writing it is not possible to say how short a course or how low a dose can be effective. It may be that even a diagnostic test of testicular testosterone responsiveness to hCG will trigger a growth spurt. Certainly, 3-6 months of an anabolic steroid in a dose of 0.05 mg/kg/24 hours may do so frequently.

The decision whether to use such treatment or not is a difficult one based on what will happen without treatment and on the psychological consequences of doing nothing. This is where the practice of medicine becomes an art rather than a science and no firm recommendations can be made at present, save to say that my own threshold for providing treatment in this highly sensitive phase of development is constantly being reduced.

DISPROPORTIONATE SHORT STATURE

The recognition of a short trunk and/or of short limbs is made easier by anthropometric measurement, but making a diagnosis subsequently is much more difficult. One absolute prerequisite is a dedicated radiologist and access to a radiological compendium (Spranger *et al* 1974). There are a number of books of reference in this field, but they all have the disadvantage of resembling most books on wild flowers in that, unless you know what you are looking for, the only possible way of using them is to leaf through, looking for the solution to a clinical problem. For this reason there is much to be said for having a small book and I find Felson's (1973) contribution helpful.

Table 4.1 Clinically recognised syndromes of disproportionate short stature. (Data from *Journal of Pediatrics* (1978) **93**, 614–6 and Parkin (1981) *British Medical Bulletin* **37**, 297–302.)

Limbs predominantly affected	Trunk and limbs affected
Achondroplasia	Achondrogenesis
Chondroplasia	Chondroectodermal dysplasia
Diastrophic dwarfism	Metatrophic dwarfism
Dyschondrosteosis	Spondyloepiphyseal dysplasias
Hypochondroplasia	Multiple endchondromatosis
Metaphyseal chondroplasias	Mucopolysaccharidoses
Multiple epiphyseal dysplasia	

I have attempted in Table 4.1 to indicate the broad categories of disorder which are recognised clinically. In practice, skeletal radiographs are needed for any child who is found to have disproportionately short limbs or trunk or both. They are needed when one of the parents is small, especially if the parental short stature is disproportionate. To detect this, it is worth measuring the sitting height of the short parents of short children as well as their stature. Finally, I would say to any reader that it is as well not to be depressed about skeletal dysplasias. They are immensely difficult and, as Silverman says in Felson's book, experts are individuals who make mistakes with confidence.

REFERENCES

AARSKOG D. (1981) Dysmorphic syndromes. In C.G.D. Brook (ed.) *Clinical Paediatric Endocrinology*, pp.159–90. Blackwell Scientific Publications, Oxford.

ABBASI V. & ALDIGE C. (1977) Evaluation of sodium L-thyroxin (T4) requirement in replacement therapy of hypothyroidism. *Journal of Pediatrics* **90**, 298-301.

ALMQVIST S. & RUNE I. (1961) Studies on sulfation factor (SF) activity of human serum. *Acta Endocrinologica* **36**, 566-76.

BERGSMA D. (1979) *Birth Defects Compendium*, 2nd edn. Macmillan, London.

BROOK C.G.D., MÜRSET G., ZACHMANN M. *et al* (1974) Growth in children with 45XO Turner syndrome. *Archives of Disease in Childhood* **49**, 789-95.

BROOK C.G.D. (1978) Disorders of the hypothalamo–pituitary axis. In *Practical Paediatric Endocrinology* pp. 49-62. Academic Press, New York.

FELSON B. (1973) Dwarfs and other little people. In *Seminars in Roentgenology* **8**, No. 2., New York.

FRIEDMAN M. & STRANG L. B. (1966) Effect of long-term corticosteroids and corticotrophin on the growth of children. *Lancet* **2**, 566-72.

FRASIER S. D., ACETO T., HAYLES A. B. & MIKITY V. (1977) Collaborative study of the effects of human growth hormone in growth hormone deficiency: IV Treatment with low doses of human growth hormone based on body weight. *Journal of Clinical Endocrinology and Metabolism* **44**, 22-31.

GRANT D. B., HAMBLEY J., BECKER D. *et al* (1973) Reduced sulphation factor in undernourished children. *Archives of Disease in Childhood* **48**, 596—600.

LACEY K. A. & PARKIN J. M. (1974) The normal short child. Community study of children in Newcastle upon Tyne. *Archives of Disease in Childhood* **49**, 417-24.

PIMSTONE B. L., BARBEZAT G., HANSEN J. D. L. *et al* (1968) Studies on growth hormone secretion in protein-calories malnutrition. *American Journal of Clinical Nutrition* **21**, 482-7.

POWELL G. F., BRASEL J. A. & BLIZZARD R. M. (1967) Emotional deprivation and growth retardation simulating idiopathic hypopituitarism. 1. Clinical evaluation of the syndrome. *New England Journal of Medicine* **276**, 1271-8.
2. (with Raiti S.) Endocrinological evaluation of the syndrome. *New Endland Journal of Medicine* **276**, 1269-83.

PRADER A., TANNER J. M. & VON HARNACH G. A. (1963) Catch-up growth following illness or starvation. *Journal of Pediatrics* **62**, 646-59.

PREECE M. A., TANNER J. M., WHITEHOUSE R. H. *et al* (1976) Dose dependence of growth response to human growth hormone in growth hormone deficiency. *Journal of Clinical Endocrinology and Metabolism* **42**, 477-83.

PREECE M. A. (1981) Growth hormone deficiency. In C. G. D. Brook (ed.) *Clinical Paediatric Endocrinology*, pp.285-304. Blackwell Scientific Publications, Oxford.

REZVANI I. & DiGEORGE A. M. (1977) Reassessment of the daily dose of oral thyroxine for replacement therapy in hypothyroid children *Journal of Pediatrics* **90**, 291 7.

RUDMAN D., KUTNER M. H., BLACKSTON R. D., CUSHMAN R. A., BAIN R. P. & PATTERSON J. H. (1981) Children with normal-variant short stature: treatment with human growth hormone for six months. *New England Journal of Medicine* **305**, 123-31.

RUSSELL A. (1954) A syndrome of intrauterine dwarfism recognisable at birth with craniofacial dysotosis, disproportionately short arms and other abnormalities. *Proceedings of the Royal Society of Medicine* **47**, 1040-4.

SHALET S. M. & BEARDWELL C. G. (1979) Endocrine consequences of treatment of malignant disease in childhood. *Journal of the Royal Society of Medicine* **72**, 39-41.

SILVER H. K. (1964) Asymmetry, short stature and variations of sexual development: a syndrome of congenital malformation. *American Journal of Diseases of Children* **107**, 495-515.

SMITH D. W. (1976) *Recognisable patterns of Human Malformation*, 2nd edn. W. B. Saunders, Philadelphia.

SPRANGER J. W., LANGER L. O. & WIDERMANN H. R. (1974) Bone Dysplasias. *An Atlas of Constitutional Disorders of Skeletal Development*. W. B. Saunders, Philadelphia.

TANNER J. M., GOLDSTEIN H. & WHITEHOUSE R. H. (1970) Standards for children's height at ages 2-9 years allowing for heights of parents. *Archives of Disease in Childhood* **45**, 755-62.

TANNER J. M., WHITEHOUSE R. H., HUGHES P. C. & VINCE F. P. (1971) Effect of human growth hormone treatment for 1 to 7 years on growth of 100 children with growth hormone deficiency, low birthweight, inherited smallness, Turner's syndrome and other complaints. *Archives of Disease in Childhood* **46**, 745-782.

TANNER J. M. (1972) Human growth hormone. *Nature* **237**, 433-9.

TANNER J. M. & WHITEHOUSE R. H. (1975) Revised standards for triceps and subscapular skinfolds in British children. *Archives of Disease in Childhood* **50**, 142-5.

TANNER J. M. LEJERRAGA H. & CAMERON N. (1975) The natural history of the Silver-Russell syndrome: a longitudinal study of 39 cases. *Pediatric Research* **9**, 611-23.

TANNER J. M. & THOMSON A. M. (1970) Standards for birth weight at gestation periods from 32-42 weeks allowing for maternal height and weight. *Archives of Disease in Childhood* **45**, 566-9.

TANNER J. M. (1978) *Fetus into man*. Open Books, London.

TENORE A., BERMAN W. F., PARKS J. S. *et al* (1977) Basal and stimulated growth hormone concentrations in inflammatory bowel disease. *Journal of Clinical Endocrinology and Metabolism* **44**, 622-8.

TURNER H. H. (1938) A syndrome of infantilism, congenital webbed neck and cubitus valgus. *Endocrinology* **23**, 566-74.

URBAN M. D., LEE P. A., DORST J. P. *et al* (1979) Oxandrolone therapy in patients with Turner syndrome. *Journal of Pediatrics* **94**, 823-7.

VANDERSCHEUREN-LODEWEYCKX M,. WOLTER R., MOLLA A. *et al* (1973) Plasma growth hormone in coeliac disease. *Helvetica Paediatrica Acta* **28**, 349-57.

VANDERSCHEUREN-LODEWEYCKX M., EGGERMONT E., CORNETTE C. *et al* (1977) Decreased serum thyroid levels and increased TSH response to TRH in infants with coeliac disease. *Clinical Endocrinology* **6**, 361-7.

VIMPANI G. V., VIMPANI A. F., LIKGARD G. P. *et al* (1977) Prevalence of severe growth hormone deficiency. *British Medical Journal* **2**, 427-30.

CHAPTER 5

The Tall Child

Summary of diagnosis and therapy-orientated management of tall stature

1 Measure child's height and parental heights.
2 Plot centile positions. Is the child tall for the parents?
3 Are there signs of puberty? If so, refer to Chapter 9.
4 Does he look normal? If not, a syndrome needs to be diagnosed.
5 Measure growth velocity. If increased, investigate and treat accordingly.
6 If growth is normal, measure skeletal maturity and do a height prediction. Decide whether or not treatment is necessary or justifiable.

Tallness in children usually presents less initial concern than shortness because, at least in early childhood, being tall is socially advantageous. Excessively tall stature may, on the other hand, cause problems at school, first because it is difficult to remember that a five-year-old who has the stature of an eight-year-old is actually five and secondly because his bulk is inappropriately large for classroom furniture and his strength disproportionately great for his peers. Thus tall children may be labelled as clumsy or aggressive and tall stature may cause many emotional problems. In adult life tallness may become socially disadvantageous, especially in the teenage years, and coping with tallness generally seems to be more of a problem for adults than coping with short stature, which is more of a problem in childhood. Finally, the diagnoses with which tall stature may be associated are in some ways more sinister than those causing short stature. Doctors see fewer tall children than small ones, so that they are often less experienced in this area.

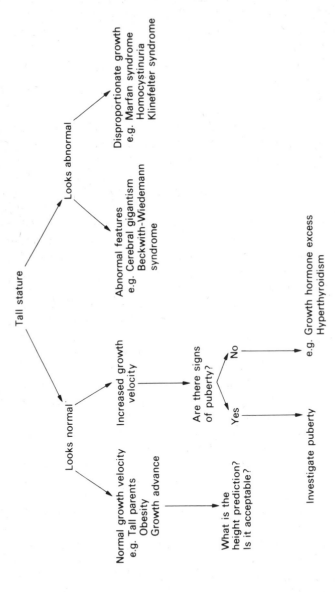

Fig. 5.1 The differential diagnosis of tall stature.

Diagnosis of tall stature (Fig. 5.1)

Many causes of tall stature are associated with early puberty and that subject will be covered in more detail in Chapter 9. If testes are enlarged or there are beginnings of breast development or of pubic hair, tall stature is probably a manifestation of early puberty or of premature androgen secretion and the cause should be sought there. Otherwise the principles of growth assessment are the means to make a diagnosis

Comparing the height of the child with the heights of the parents is done in exactly the same way as it is for short stature. Often, however, tall parents bring up the problem on account of their own stature, rather than because their child seems out of place. In dealing with short stature, parents worry about their child and are often relatively surprised to find how short they are themselves. A child who is tall for his or her parents may or may not have a problem now and may or may not have a problem later. It is in dealing with both of these that we must be concerned. Whether or not the child has a physical problem now can be discovered by clinical examination for dysmorphic features and by measuring growth velocity.

Dysmorphic features and tall stature

Most of the tall stature syndromes are rare and fewer in number than those associated with short stature. The Marfan syndrome (Fig. 5.2) is one of the most frequent and comprises the triad of excessively long limbs, especially arachnodactyly, ocular abnormalities (a tendency to subluxation of the lens, myopia and retinal detachment), and cardiovascular problems manifesting in childhood as a valve lesion. The aneurysmal problems associated with the Marfan syndrome rarely present in childhood. Although it is inherited as an autosomal dominant trait, patients may arise as a result of fresh mutations and, as the expressivity of gene varies within and between families, a positive family history is not a requisite for the diagnosis. The Marfan syndrome is diagnosed clinically and there is no investigation which is diagnostic. Long limbs and dislocated lenses also occur in homocystinuria but here mental retardation is a feature and homocystine is found in the urine. Congenital contractural arachnodactyly, another variant of the Marfan syndrome, is associated with scoliosis and multiple congenital joint contractures. In this condition

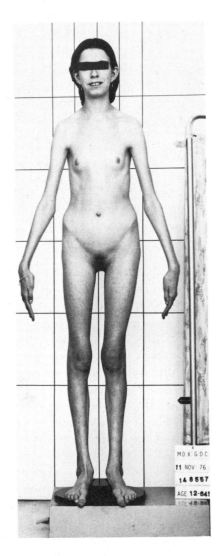

Fig. 5.2
The Marfan syndrome.

cardiovascular and ocular manifestations are not usual.

Cerebral gigantism (Sotos syndrome) usually presents early in childhood with tall stature, large hands and feet, mild mental retardation and general clumsiness. Bone age is usually advanced and puberty occurs early so ultimate tall stature is not generally a problem and the patients may end up by being rather short.

A rare but well known syndrome because of its association with hypoglycaemia is the Beckwith-Wiedemann syndrome where macroglossia and exomphalos are associated with large size and islet cell hyperplasia leading to hyperinsulinaemia and hypoglycaemia. In a few patients who have survived to adult life, the final height has been around 97th centile. Occasionally, the phacomatoses (neurofibromatosis, tuberous sclerosis, etc.) present with tall stature alone, but more often they are associated with early puberty and the cutaneous manifestations should be immediately apparent. Where a tall child has dysmorphic features, the use of text books of dysmorphology is recommended.

One cause of long-leggedness associated with being tall for parental heights is Klinefelter syndrome. In this condition, tall stature for the parents is associated with a normal growth velocity, long legs from childhood (Schibler *et al* 1974), small testes and performance in school which is not as good as it should be for the family. Most cases are not diagnosed until adult life when they present with hypogonadism or infertility, but the tall stature may be a feature especially when testicular function at puberty fails to bring adequate sexual development and allows growth to continue at a normal rate resulting in extremely tall stature. Fig. 5.3 shows the growth velocity of boys with Klinefelter syndrome continuing without a pubertal spurt well beyond the normal age. In the clinical management of these patients it is important not to confuse the family about the chromosomal abnormality: in one case with which I have been associated, the parents of a patient with Klinefelter syndrome were under the impression that the additional chromosome material would inevitably cause gender identification problems, homosexuality at best and a sex change at puberty at worst. The occurrence of gynaecomastia (Fig. 5.4) at puberty may disastrously reinforce this impression. Gynaecomastia may occur in any situation where there is a relative poverty of testosterone in puberty but it may also occur in perfectly normal adolescence. Occasionally, when it becomes marked, it is a cause of great distress. Most cases disappear spontaneously but where gynaecomastia is a cause of great psychological distress, subareolar mastectomy produces instant cure and is probably preferable to trials of drug therapy with anti-oestrogen compounds, such as tamoxifen. Where there is time for such treatment, it is probably better to await spontaneous cure.

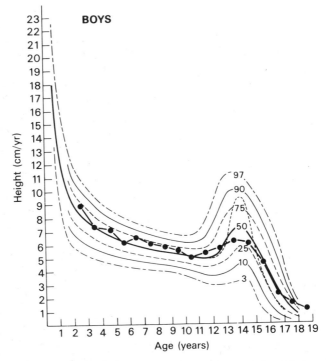

Fig. 5.3 Height velocity of boys with Klinefelter syndrome. Reproduced with permission (Schibler *et al* 1974).

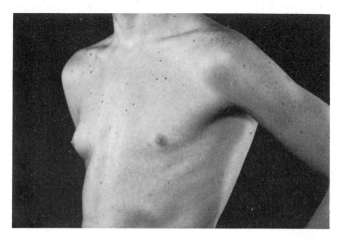

Fig. 5.4 Gynaecomastia at puberty in a boy with Klinefelter syndrome.

In many tall children feet appear disproportionately large because feet reach adult size before the rest of the body. There are cases, however, where ordinary High Street stores cannot cater for excessively large feet and shoes must be sought in shops specialising in large sizes. In the Marfan syndrome, feet really are disproportionately large and in this situation a bespoke shoemaker can sometimes help, although at a price. On one occasion I have had to seek orthopaedic help to shorten the extremely long first metatarsal bones of a girl with the Marfan syndrome (Fig. 5.2) for whom shoes were neither available nor cosmetically acceptable. The result of operation was very satisfactory.

Increased growth velocity

When growth proceeds at a persistently increased rate, an explanation has to be forthcoming. There are three glands that have to be considered in this context, the hypothalamo-pituitary axis, the thyroid, and the adrenal gland.

Gigantism due to disorders of the hypothalamo-pituitary axis and resulting usually from a space-occupying lesion in the pituitary is rare in childhood. The hallmarks of the diagnosis are a raised basal level of growth hormome, a loss of diurnal rhythm, and a paradoxical rise of growth hormone following a glucose load. This calls for neuroradiological investigation and treatment of the pituitary tumor.

For reasons which are obscure, hyperthyroidism in childhood is less common on the eastern side of the Atlantic ocean, compared to the western side. Thyroid antibodies occur with equal frequency on both sides and Hashimoto's thyroiditis is a common cause of hypothyroidism in children in England. It is unlikely that the relative paucity of hyperthyroidism is due to want of looking for it, for when it does occur it is obvious. The reason may lie in the increased iodine intake from fortified foods in North America.

To make a diagnosis and to manage hyperthyroidism it is important to have access to measurements of tri-iodothyronine (T3) because its rise in thyrotoxicosis precedes that of thyroxin (T4) and because its level is a much more sensitive predictor of response to treatment. The measurements of free levels of T3 and T4 are also valuable, especially when there may be abnormality of levels of thyroxin-binding proteins. Since we have been measuring these, abnormalities leading to both high and low levels of bound thyroid hormones have appeared to be quite common: measurement of free hormone concentrations avoids management errors (R.P. Ekins & A.B. Kurtz, personal communication). Treatment of thyrotoxicosis should be medical in the first instance but the option of thyroidectomy should be considered in patients with thyrotoxicosis which is not fully under control within twelve months (Parks 1981). The chief disadvantage may be the induction of hypothyroidism but that is much more easily managed and anyway most patients with thyrotoxicosis will probably eventually require thyroxin supplementation.

Adrenal disease usually draws attention to itself by the appearance of pubic hair and growth of the phallus in either sex. At first, however, increased growth velocity may be the only complaint. This must not be dismissed as part of an early puberty unless *all* the signs are compatible. Pubic hair in the absence of breast development in girls or testicular enlargement in boys should be regarded with suspicion. It is not frankly pathological, but markedly increased height velocity is not the usual concomitant of physiological early adrenarche. In this situation the differential diagnosis lies between congenital adrenal hyperplasia and some sort of functioning adrenal tumour, either benign or malignant. While growth arrest and glucocorticoid oversecretion are the pointers to a diagnosis of Cushing syndrome of hypothalamo-pituitary origin, androgen oversecretion is usually indicative of adrenal pathology. Investigation of these conditions is covered in detail in textbooks of paediatric endocrinology (Forest 1981).

'Simple' tall stature

A persistently raised growth rate is the signal to a problem for immediate solution. The assessment of skeletal maturity indicates whether there will be a problem later and, indeed, whether it is soluble. Fig. 5.5 illustrates this point. The mother of the two girls in question is fairly tall (180 cm, well above the 97th centile) but remembers her own adolescence and early adult life as being ruined by her early acquisition of tall stature. Having found a tall man for a husband she feared that her daughters might be worse off than she. Accordingly, she brought her older daughter to see me at the age of 9.6 years. At that time Eleanor was certainly tall and there were no pubertal signs. Her bone age was 10.8 years, which means that about 86% of her growth had taken place (Bayley & Pinneau 1952). Using the prediction Table A10 of Tanner *et al* (1975), her final stature could be calculated as follows:

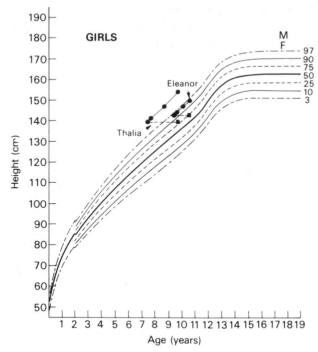

Fig. 5.5 'Simple' tall stature.

Height prediction
= (height × 0.92) − (chronological age × 3.8)
− (bone age* × 2.3) + constant (99)
= (142.6 × 0.92) − (9.6 × 3.8) − (10.8 × 2.3) + 99
= 131.2 − 36.5 − 24.8 + 99
= 168.9

Thus it was possible to indicate that Eleanor was unlikely to have a problem.

To the same consultation came sister Thalia. She was taller but was not as fortunate as her sister in the (proportionate) advance of bone age. Consequently the sums in her case gave a height prediction in the region of 180 cm and it is she who may have her mother's problem. Repeated height predictions will need be done to confirm her likely final height.

* Radius, ulna and short bones according to Tanner (1975)

Ultimate tall stature is something which treatment can prevent. By pharmacologically advancing bone age growth potential can be lost, thus taking advantage of what can be a disastrous mistake in the case of short people. This applies regardless of diagnosis and in some situations may forestall other problems, usually of behaviour.

Treatment of tall stature

An increased growth velocity requires diagnosis and appropriate treatment. It is not my purpose to review treatment of endocrine disease here.

An excessive growth prognosis may also require treatment. What constitutes excessive is not a matter in which the opinion of the doctor is necessarily relevant. Nevertheless, because all treatments involve risk, boys should not be treated unless their final height is going to be comfortably in excess of 190 cm, 175 cm (the 75th centile for boys) being the level below which I believe treatment in girls may be described as meddlesome. Many tall children with tall parents will be quite happy with final heights considerably in excess of these.

Treatment for girls comprises the administration of oestrogen in the form of ethinyloestradiol 300μg given daily continuously, together with norethisterone 10 mg daily for five days at the end of each monthly cycle to promote endometrial shedding. This produces growth in breasts and pubic hair and usually temporarily increases growth velocity. The mechanism of action of oestrogen in reducing growth prognosis is obscure, but when applied prepubertally it does produce worthwhile results (Wettenhall et al 1975, Zachmann et al 1975). The dangers of hypertension, thrombophlebitis, emboli, liver damage, vaginal carcinoma, etc., which are associated with the administration of oestrogens are well known, but have not been found in clinical practice in this situation (Wettenhall 1981). Nevertheless, they must be borne in mind as must be the great variation in response to therapy, which is extremely difficult to predict. It is not a treatment to be recommended with impunity — and yet the psychological boost which the onset of therapy may give may make all other considerations seem minor by comparison. Amenorrhoea is unusual after withdrawal of therapy in girls. Jacobs *et al* (1977) have pointed out that most of the problems which occur after the withdrawal of the oral contraceptive pill antedate its start and are not caused by treatment. The same is presumably true in this case.

In boys, testosterone oenanthate given in a dose of 250 mg every two to four weeks seems to be more effective than oestrogen in girls (Zachmann *et al* 1976). The increase in growth velocity is striking at the start of therapy and patients should be warned of this. In a very few instances, behaviour problems may occur with testosterone treatment but my impression is that these are generally associated with the reason for giving the treatment in the first place rather than the result of it. For the most part, treatment in boys is relatively freer of risk than in girls, with the possible exception of long-term consequences on sex hormone production. Testicular size reduces during treatment with testosterone but recovery is generally complete. The theoretical hazard of Leydig cell atrophy nonetheless remains and treatment should probably not be continuous for too long.

When to institute medical treatment has to be based on chronological age, bone age, pubertal status and height prediction. It must be remembered that actual height cannot be lost so treatment must be begun in time for there to be enough height left to shorten. In other words, treatment only affects height to come, so the younger the (bone) age at the start of treatment the more effect will rapid advance in skeletal maturity have on the time left for growth. As treatment necessarily involves pubertal induction or acceleration, it should not be instituted before (chronological) age ten and preferably not before eleven. It does not seem logical to start treatment at a given height, irrespective of the other parameters, although some authors do suggest this. This must be an area when individual circumstances dictate the cause of action and when an experienced physician may need to advise.

Surgical treatment of tall stature is not recommended. Orthopaedic operations can go wrong and the consequences of this happening to a tall but healthy person are such that it is not worth the risk. Here, if anywhere, prevention is better than cure but, as in all growth problems, early intervention is required. Tall children cannot lose height they have already gained, they can only lose growth potential.

REFERENCES

BAYLEY N. & PINNEAU S.R. (1952) Table for predicting adult height from skeletal age revised for use with the Greulich-Pyle hand standards. *Journal of Pediatrics* **40**, 423-41. (Erratum **41**, 371).

FOREST M. G. (1981) Adrenal steroid excess. In C.G.D. Brook (ed.) *Clinical Paediatric Endocrinology,* pp. 429-52. Blackwell Scientific Publications, Oxford.

JACOBS H.S., KNUTH V.A., HULL M.G.R. *et al* (1977) Post-pill amenorrhoea — cause or co-incidence? *British Medical Journal* **2**, 940-2.

PARKS J.S. (1981) Hyperthyroidism. In C.G.D. Brook (ed.), *Clinical Paediatric Endocrinology,* pp. 340-65, Blackwell Scientific Publications, Oxford.

SCHIBLER D., BROOK C.G.D., KIND H.P. *et al* (1974) Growth and body proportions in 54 boys and men with Klinefelter syndrome. *Helvetica Paediatrica Acta* **29**, 325-33.

TANNER J.M., WHITEHOUSE R.H., MARSHALL W.A. *et al* (1975) Assessment of skeletal maturity and prediction of adult height. Academic Press, New York.

WETTENHALL H.N.B., CAHILL C. & ROCHE A.F. (1975) Tall girls: a survey of 15 years of management and treatment. *Journal of Pediatrics* **86**, 602-10.

WETTENHALL H.N.B. (1981) The tall child. In C.G.D. Brook (ed.), *Clinical Paediatric Endocrinology,* pp. 134-40. Blackwell Scientific Publications, Oxford.

ZACHMANN M., FERRANDEZ A., MÜRSET G. *et al* (1975) Oestrogen treatment of excessively tall girls. *Helvetica Paediatrica Acta* **30**, 11-30.

ZACHMANN M., FERRANDEZ A., MÜRSET G. *et al* (1976) Testosterone treatment of excessively tall boys. *Journal of Pediatrics* **88**, 116-23.

CHAPTER 6

The Fat Child

Summary of diagnosis and therapy-orientated management of obesity in childhood

1   Is the child fat? Measure skinfold thicknesses and compare with standard charts.
2   Measure child's height and parental heights and plot on centile charts. Does the child resemble the parents in size and shape?
3   Is the child tall for age and for parents? If so, chances of pathology are very small.
4   Is the child small? If so, there may be an endocrine cause for obesity.
5   Is the child mentally retarded? If so, short stature may be associated with obesity and mental retardation in one of the syndromes of obesity.
6   Is medical intervention indicated? If so, dietary advice is needed and time in helping the family to adhere to it.

Obesity is so common in our population that a doctor can make it more or less a part of his clinical practice as he chooses to define it and as his zeal takes him. Like other growth disorders there is no absolute threshold where abnormality takes over from extremes of normality.

Does obesity matter?

There is general agreement from life insurance experience, that at all ages in adult life obesity is associated with increased rates of mortality and that the level of mortality varies more or less in proportion to the degree of obesity. Death occurs mainly from cardiovascular disease, but also from diabetes mellitus (Office of Health Economics 1969). The question is whether it is the obesity *per se* that is the culprit or whether it makes its contribution through its associations with hypertension, physical inactivity, increased levels of serum triglyceride, impaired glucose tolerance and hyperinsulinaemia with insulin resistance (Shaper & Marr 1977).

In considering the influence of nutrition on the origins of coronary heart disease, the interaction of quality of diet with quantity makes any discussion extremely hard to interpret (Brook 1978). Shaper & Marr (1977) came to a reasonable conclusion: 'No-one will question that gross obesity is unhealthy and few will argue the association between weight and many established and some possible risk factors for coronary heart disease. Nevertheless, the available evidence does not suggest that obesity in adult life should be the prime target for action designed to prevent coronary heart disease'.

What about children?

Much work has been done to answer the key question in this field which is whether patterns of fatness established during childhood persist into adult life. It is becoming increasingly clear that few fat babies remain fat by five years of age (Poskitt & Cole 1977, Sveger 1978). On the other hand Charney *et al* (1976) reported that infant weight did seem to correlate with weight in adult life. Since height can be predicted in childhood and since the major component of weight is lean body mass, even in the very obese, this was not surprising. But the risk of being overweight in adult life is nonetheless related to the degree of overweight in childhood, although only 7% and 13% of 26-year-old overweight men and women in one study had been overweight at the age of seven (Stark *et al* 1981). This study suggested that overweight children were more likely to remain overweight than their contemporaries of norm. weight were to become overweight, but that excessive weight gain might begin at any time.

Hawk & Brook (1979a) first reported the influence of childhood skinfold thickness on adult values; their study was specifically designed to obviate the criticism that overweight and obesity are not necessarily synonymous. Skinfold thicknesses were measured on 318 boys and 303 girls aged 3–15 years and the measurements were repeated 15 years later. Childhood values of skinfold thickness were found to predict adult values very poorly, especially when compared to the childhood prediction of adult height. Values for correlation of weight were intermediate between height and skinfold thickness. The number of even somewhat obese children in our study was small and there are at present no long-term skinfold studies of obese children. My conclusion is that moderate obesity in childhood constitutes a social and cosmetic problem (and not less important for that), but not a reason for intervention on medical grounds in the absence of other compounding problems.

Determination of body fatness

Family likenesses in body fatness are commonly observed and well documented (Garn & Clark 1976) but families share not only genes in common, they also share environmental circumstances. The separation of the genetic and environmental contributions to the determination of body fatness has been extremely difficult. Twin studies have tended to suggest that genetic influences make the strongest contribution (Borjeson 1976, Brook *et al* 1975), but our recent experience has been sobering (Hawk & Brook 1979b). In a study of skinfold thicknesses in parents and their children, amongst whom were monozygotic and dizygotic twins, correlations of skinfold thicknesses between parents and their adult offspring were not significant, nor were sibling correlations. But twins, especially monozygotic ones, had lifestyles that were so exceedingly similar that analyses of their skinfold thicknesses alone would have led to directly contradictory conclusions. It is clear that twin data have to be regarded with a high degree of suspicion since twins have much more than genes in common. As children they are treated more alike and as adults they behave more alike, even when they live apart, than do siblings. There is little doubt that environmental influences are paramount in the determination of body fatness.

Assessment of body fatness

Definitions of fatness and particularly definitions of obesity, based on weight-for-height, are necessarily indirect and are unsatisfactory for many reasons. Variations of weight are greatest at both extremes of the height range (Newens & Goldstein 1972), which may mean that obese children are either tall or small, which is reasonable, but, once again, overweight and obesity are not synonymous.

The weight of a tall child is usually compared for purposes of assessment with the median weight of an older child of the same height. Body fatness does not change with age as height does, so such comparisons may be badly misleading at times when the rates of change are conspicuously discrepant. The prepubertal fat spurt in boys contrasts strongly with the prepubertal deceleration in height velocity.

The density of triglyceride is 0.8. There has, therefore, to be a very considerable increase in fat volume before change in weight adequately reflects it. Nor do sequential changes in weight help much. The loss of lean body mass and water during starvation occurs both in adults (Runcie & Hilditch 1974) and children (Brook et al 1974) and weight changes on diet may reflect this as much as changes in body fatness. Direct measurements of body fatness are therefore needed for any proper assessment, and the choices in practice lie between measurements of limb circumference and of skinfold thickness. Physical methods, such as X-rays, ultrasound, densitometry, dilution techniques, estimation of whole body potassium and so on, are obviously inappropriate to everyday practice. Measurements of limb circumference suffer from being combination measurements (fat, muscle and bone) and they are difficult to perform repeatedly. For any study

of clinical nutrition, skinfold thickness measurements are
required (see Chapter 3). A combination of triceps and
subscapular skinfolds has been shown to be representative
of total body fat (Parizkova & Roth 1972) and to show the
least between observer error (Womersley & Durnin 1973).

CHILDHOOD OBESITY IN CLINICAL PRACTICE

For the most part, obesity in children arises incidentally as
a clinical problem, usually in association with a respiratory
tract infection. Obese children undoubtedly get more
respiratory tract infections than non-obese children, but
with lower social class biasing an increased incidence of
obesity this may well not be cause and effect. Whether
anything ought to be done about such a problem depends
entirely upon the degree of obesity. I am inclined not to be
overzealous in mild cases.

   The child who presents with obesity as a complaint is
different. The obvious first step is to exclude other causes
of obesity and all are well taught to, but seldom seen, by
doctors. Cushing syndrome, hypothyroidism, the various
types of pseudohypoparathyroidism, hypopituitarism and
hypothalamic tumours are all associated with obesity, but
obesity is rarely the presenting feature. All these conditions
are associated with short stature, whereas overnutrition
tends to be associated with overgrowth of the lean tissues
(Cheek *et al* 1970). The chance of an obese child who is tall
for his or her age and parents having endocrine disease is
small. When the child is short this is not the case. Nor is it
the case when the child is mentally retarded. Often mental
retardation and short stature occur together with obesity
and this is a signal for a different type of diagnosis.

The obesity syndromes

The fat boy in the *Pickwick Papers* of Charles Dickens has
generally been regarded as a source of amusement but
somnolence in obesity is a grave sign, for it originates

Table 6.1 Causes of obesity in childhood.

Aetiology	Examples	Comment
Dysmorphic, possibly sometimes genetically determined	Prader–Willi syndrome Laurence-Moon-Biedl syndrome Down syndrome	Conditions characterised by short stature and mental retardation
Endocrine	Hypothalamic disorder, injury, or space-occupying lesion	Conditions mostly characterised by short stature
	Hypopituitarism, especially GH deficiency	
	Hypogonadotrophic hypogonadism	
	Hypogonadism	
	Cushing syndrome	
	Hypothyroidism	
	Pseudohypoparathyroidism	Patients may present with fits
	Hyperinsulinaemia Beckwith–Wiedemann syndrome Insulinoma	Associated with hypoglycaemia. Patients may be tall
Nutritional	'Simple obesity'	Characterised by tall stature and advanced bone age
Inactivity		Associated with mental retardation or physical disability (e.g. spinabifida)
Iatrogenic	Psychotropic drugs Corticosteroids	
Socioeconomic	Low social class Ethnic group	

either from carbon dioxide narcosis or from a hypothalamic lesion. Short stature is a pointer to such a lesion and to many of the syndromes of obesity. Psychomotor developmental retardation, even if it is not the cause of the obesity, is made so much worse by it that this too is a condition to seek. Table 6.1 which is based on the work of Bray (1978), indicates the major obesity syndromes.

The *Prader-Willi* syndrome may often be diagnosed at birth through the extreme hypotonia and feeding problems of early infancy. In childhood, physical features of extreme obesity with mental retardation and a

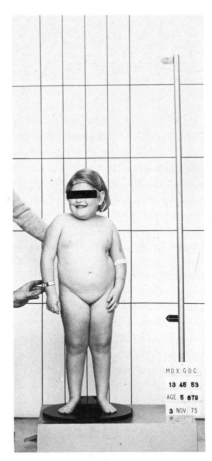

Fig. 6.1
Prader-Willi syndrome.

characteristic facies (Fig. 6.1) become obvious. These patients have a number of very serious problems. The first is their insatiable appetite which may lead to the kitchen and larder becoming something of a fortress. Secondly, while short stature is not an invariable accompaniment in early childhood, the maintenance of high food intake may be found to be necessary for normal growth in some individuals. Calorie restriction, although it is very difficult, may be associated with growth failure. Thirdly, calorie restriction may need to be extreme to produce any result and, in these situations, growth failure is almost inevitable. Fourthly, although maturity onset diabetes is associated with obesity in all instances, it is particularly associated with the Prader–Willi syndrome and this may be because the pancreas of these patients is less able to maintain insulin production. Finally, scoliosis is a not infrequent problem and the combination of gross obesity and scoliosis may well lead to respiratory failure and death.

The *Laurence-Moon-Biedl* syndrome is much less common and is characterised by polydactyly and retinitis pigmentosa. The *Beckwith-Wiedemann* syndrome generally presents in the newborn period with macrosomia and hypoglycaemia. Obesity is a problem of later childhood.

Endocrine problems

Hypothalamic obesity is not common, but is is of special interest for the light it sheds on the origins of the obese state. There is considerable evidence to suggest that insulin plays a major role in the establishment of hypothalamic obesity (Martin 1978). Vagotomy reverses the syndrome of hypothalamic obesity (Inoue & Bray 1977). The hyperinsulinaemia of obesity is a well established phenomenon and it now appears that the insulin resistance of obesity is consequent on a decrease in the number of insulin receptors on the fat cell when insulin is circulating in large amounts (Bar *et al* 1978). Fig. 6.2, based on these data, illustrates how the obese state may be maintained; only

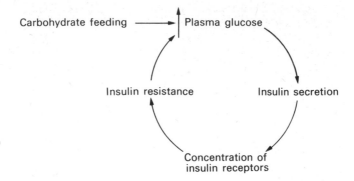

Fig. 6.2 Hyperinsulinaemia in obesity and the maintenance of insulin resistance.

reduction of carbohydrate feeding or prevention of insulin release in response to carbohydrate feeding will interrupt the vicious circle. The effect of such action may be judged by the precipitate fall in plasma insulin levels which follows the introduction of a low calorie diet and which long precedes significant changes in weight, body fat mass, or adipose cell size (Brook & Lloyd 1973).

Growth hormone deficiency is certainly associated with obesity but the short stature is, of course, generally the presenting feature. As Fig. 6.3 shows, the fat of growth hormone deficiency has a rather special appearance being marbled in a way that the fat of simple obesity is not. It is certainly true that there are fewer very large fat cells in patients with growth hormone deficiency (Brook 1973) but whether this appearance has anything to do with fat cell size is not known. In patients with panhypopituitarism and especially with hypogonadotrophic hypogonadism, obesity seems to be a very serious problem. Often such instances follow surgery (Fig. 6.4) and it can be very difficult to control the appetite in this situation, just as in the Prader-Willi syndrome. Hypogonadism maybe associated with obesity but this is probably due more to the emotional problems than to the endocrine one. Growth hormone treatment in growth hormone deficient subjects leads to a loss of skinfold thickness but this is only temporary and

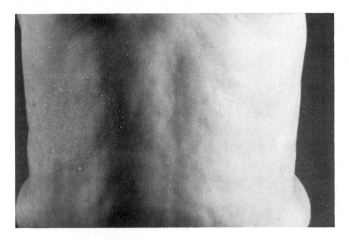

Fig. 6.3 *(above)*
Characteristic
appearance of fat
in growth hormone
deficiency.

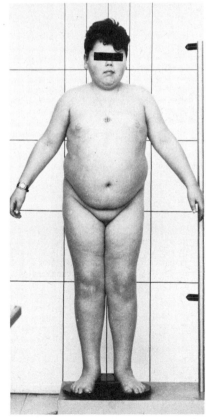

Fig. 6.4
Panhypopituitarism,
hypogonadotrophic
hypogonadism and
obesity after cranial
surgery in a twelve-
year-old.

there is a gradual increase over succeeding years of treatment unless dietary efforts are made to keep the situation in control. Growth hormone mainly affects the growth of legs in puberty whereas sex steroids affect the growth of the trunk and treatment of hypogonadism may considerably improve the cosmetic appearance, again without making very much difference to the absolute skinfold thickness.

The other endocrine syndromes generally present with the characteristic medical features rather than with obesity *per se*. Pseudohypoparathyroidism may be an exception in this instance and the resemblance of patients with this

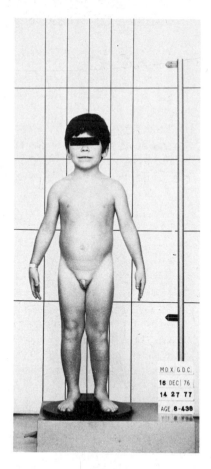

Fig. 6.5 Pseudo-hypoparathyroidism.

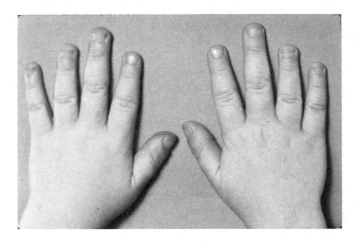

Fig. 6.6 Characteristic appearance of hands in pseudohypo-parathyroidism.

condition (Fig. 6.5) and the characteristic early fusion of their metacarpals which leads to an abnormal appearance of the hands (Fig. 6.6), are worth seeking in any short obese child, particularly if there is mental retardation.

It is not the purpose of this chapter to describe the investigation of the various neuroendocrine causes of obesity, but the short obese child or the obese child with delayed bone age deserves more than a passing thought. Details of investigation can be found in a standard textbook of paediatric endocrinology (Brook 1981).

Mental retardation is frequently accompanied by obesity in children. This may be because both have their origin in one of the dysmorphic syndromes, in which case short stature is a frequent concomitant. It may also be the result of the emotional pressure which the presence of a mentally retarded child puts on family dynamics. Facile though this statement is as an expression of aetiology, the contribution of obesity to the physical handicap of a mentally retarded child is abundantly evident. As such it deserves special recognition.

Management of the obese child

Starving people lose weight. The corollary is also presumed
to be true, that a person who does not lose weight is not
starving sufficiently. The final adverb is crucial here
because obese people do not necessarily eat excessively to
remain obese. That their caloric intake must have exceeded
their energy expenditure at some stage is inevitable, but in
the steady state both may be low. Consequently, some
obese people, and this includes obese children, may have to
eat extremely little if they wish to lose weight. It has been
possible to observe a child on a metabolic ward failing to
lose weight on a 250 calorie diet. The management of the
obese child is anything but simple.

The first decision is whom to treat. Preventive dietetic
advice for their unborn infant should, I believe, be offered
to the obese expectant mother and father. It should also be
positively offered to families and children with mental or
physical handicap, to families in which children receive
corticosteroid therapy, and to those in whom obesity is a
cause of (usually respiratory) morbidity. It should be
offered to those who are aggregating risk factors for
coronary heart disease (especially hypertension) and it
should be freely available for parents and children who ask
for it. There is, however, little point in offering help to any
who do not require it on medical grounds, or who do not
positively wish for it. The evidence that fat people come to
harm is insufficient to justify the time and energy involved
in their conversion to thinness.

The second question is how to treat. There are two main
alternative courses of action, which suit different people
differently. The first is the rigid regimen favoured by
commercial enterprises. The second is general dietetic
advice. Table 6.2 shows the distressingly small amounts of
food which constitute a caloric intake which will generally
produce weight loss in children. Individuals differ in how
they find it easiest to adhere to such caloric intake and
follow-up is, of course, the key to success. Physicians will
differ in their zeal for follow-up and so will their results.

Two aids to initial success are the measurement of
skinfold thickness, which is much more rewarding than

Table 6.2   800 calorie diet.

---

3 small servings of meat (including lean bacon or ham, chicken, liver and kidney), egg, cheese or fish grilled, boiled, stewed or roast

1 very small potato
Unlimited vegetables which grow above the ground

360 ml of milk; unlimited low calorie drinks

1 thin slice of bread or 2 crispbreads

2 apples, pears, oranges or peaches, or 4 satsumas, plums or apricots, or 2 slices of melon or small bananas

---

weight, and the detection of ketonuria as spur to achievement. In the long-term boredom with the diet is the great problem and a very helpful book in this respect is *Cooking to Make Kids Slim* (Ellis 1976) which provides variety in a calorie-restricted diet. Long-term results of treatment, however, are uniformly disappointing and once a patient knows what to do to lose weight, he or she is best left to organise their own life, always assuming that they do not have one of the positive medical reasons for requiring treatment. In this situation, the onus remains on the doctor.

CONCLUSION

Obesity is common in childhood, but the evidence that it does children very much harm or that it is a significant pointer to adult obesity is wanting. Body fatness is largely environmentally determined, so that general dietetic advice to the population is probably more useful than individual homilies. Some children, particularly the short and the mentally retarded, have a cause for their obesity and their obesity is an additional physical handicap. For these children, but probably for these children alone, specific investigation and treatment is required on medical grounds. For the rest of the obese population the decision about what to do is probably not a medical one.

REFERENCES

BAR R.S., HARRISON L.C., ROTH J., *et al* (1978) Insulin receptors in obesity. In Cacciari E., Laron Z. & Raiti S. (eds.), *Obesity in Childhood, Proceedings of the Serono Symposia* 17, pp. 165–77 Academic Press, New York.

BORJESON M. (1976) Aetiology of obesity in children. *Acta Paediatrica Scandinavica* **65**, 279–87.

BRAY G.A. (1978) They syndromes of childhood obesity. In Cacciari E., Laron Z. & Raiti S. (eds.),*Obesity in Childhood, Proceedings of the Serono Symposia,* **17**, 135–44. Academic Press, New York.

BROOK C.G.D. (1973) Effect of Human Growth Hormone treatment on adipose tissue in children. *Archives of Disease in Childhood* **48**, 725–8.

BROOK C.G.D. & LLOYD J.K. (1973) Adipose cell size and glucose tolerance in obese children and effects of diet. *Archives of Disease in Childhood* **48**, 301--4.

BROOK C.G.D., LLOYD J.K. & WOLFF O.H. (1974) Rapid weight loss in children. *British Medical Journal* **3**, 44–5.

BROOK C.G.D., HUNTLEY R.M.C. & SLACK J. (1975) Influence of heredity and environment in determination of skinfold thickness in children. *British Medical Journal* **2**, 719–21.

BROOK C.G.D. (1978) Influence of nutrition in childhood on the origins of coronary heart disease. *Postgraduate Medical Journal* **54**, 17J–4.

BROOK C.G.D. (1981) *Clinical Paediatric Endocrinology.* Blackwell Scientific Publications, Oxford.

CHARNEY E., GOODMAN H.C., MCBRIDE M. *et al* (1976) Childhood antecedents of adult obesity. *New England Journal of Medicine* **295**, 6–9.

CHEEK D.B., SHULTZ R.B., PARRA A. *et al* (1970) Overgrowth of lean and adipose tissue in adolescent obesity.*Pediatric Research* **4**, 268–79.

ELLIS A. (1976) *Cooking to Make Kids Slim.* Stanley Paul, London.

GARN S.M. & CLARK D.C. (1976) Trends in fatness and the origins of obesity. *Pediatrics* **57**, 443–56.

HAWK L.J. & BROOK C.G.D. (1979a) Influence of body fatness in childhood on fatness in adult life. *British Medical Journal* **1**, 151–2.

HAWK L.J. & BROOK C.G.D. (1979b) Family resemblances of height, weight and body fatness. *Archives of Disease in Childhood* **54**, 877–9.

INOUE S. & BRAY G.A. (1977) The effects of subdiaphragmatic vagotomy in rats with ventromedial hypothalamic obesity. *Endocrinology* **100**, 108–14.

MARTIN J.M. (1978) Neurohumoral regulation of insulin secretion, and glucose utilization. In Cacciari E., Laron Z. & Raiti S. (eds.), *Obesity in Childhood, Proceedings of the Serono Symposia,* **17**, 7–18. Academic Press, New York.

NEWENS E.M. & GOLDSTEIN H. (1972) Height, weight and the assessment of obesity in children. *British Journal of Preventative and Social Medicine* **26**, 33–9.

OFFICE OF HEALTH ECONOMICS. (April 1969) Obesity and Disease. *Studies in Current Health Problems* **30**, 3–32.

PARIZKOVA J. & ROTH Z. (1972) Assessment of depot fat in children from skinfold thickness measurements by Holtain caliper. *Annals of Human Biology* **44**, 613-20.

POSKITT E.M.E. & COLE T.J. (1977) Do fat babies stay fat? *British Medical Journal* **1**, 7-9.

RUNCIE J. & HILDITCH J.E. (1974) Energy provision, tissue utilisation and weight loss in prolonged starvation. *British Medical Journal* **2**, 353-6.

SHAPER A.G. & MARR J.W. (1977) Dietary recommendations for the community towards postponement of coronary heart disease. *British Medical Journal* **1**, 867-71.

STARK O., ATKINS E., WOLFF O.H. *et al* (1981) Longitudinal study of obesity in the National Survey of Health and Development. *British Medical Journal* **283**, 13-7.

SVEGER T. (1978) Does over-nutrition or obesity during the first year affect weight at age 4? *Acta Paediatrica Scandinavica* **67**, 465-7.

WOMERSLEY J. & DURNIN J.V.G.A. (1973) An experimental study on variability of measurements of skinfold thickness on young adults. *Annals of Human Biology* **45**, 281-92

CHAPTER 7

The Thin Child

Summary of diagnosis and therapy-orientated management of thinness in childhood

1 Is this child thin? Measure skinfold thicknesses and compare with standard charts. If so, are there physical signs other than thinness?
2 Measure growth velocity. If the child is growing normally there is probably nothing to be done.
3 If growth velocity is low, seek signs of organic or psychiatric disease and treat.
4 Is treatment feasible?

As far as adults are concerned, thinness is at a premium for fashion in the late twentieth century. It has not always been so and certainly is not as far as children are concerned. The giving of food to children must be amongst the most basic of human needs: the reward in seeing a healthy, happy child is sufficient in itself, but such children are traditionally displayed as having fat, round cheeks and as being soft and cuddly.

To have a child who is the reverse of all this is to advertise poverty of maternal care to the world. Food refusal by a child carries a threat of thinness and is one of the most effective insults a child can aim at its parents. Which mother of adolescent girls has never worried that her daughter eats too little or too much? Thin children are a source of great anxiety, both covert and overt, to their parents.

Medically significant thinness

Just as obesity is indefinable, so a single observation of

thinness means relatively little by itself. Coupled with short stature, it may well indicate a problem; associated with hirsutism and amenorrhoea it may be the major sign of anorexia nervosa; with an abdominal mass, the cachexia of advanced malignant disease may be suspected. A trend towards increasing thinness, however, is quite different.

After the loss of skinfold thickness between infancy and the pre-school years there is a steady increase up to the seventh decade. After age of 60, skinfold thicknesses reduce, but if they do so between, say, ages 7 and 60 there has to be a reason. It may be an unimportant one (e.g. the dictates of fashion or the cost of tailoring alterations) but an explanation is required.

In childhood, weight and weight changes are a bad guide to the elucidation of a problem of thinness. Reference to a standard centile chart indicates that between ages 2 and 10 the boy gaining weight along the 50th centile gains 17.6 kg. His third centile peer gains 13 kg. This means that a normally gaining boy achieves a weight difference of 2.2 kg per year, 180 g per month. With water flux alone accounting for, say, 2 kg per day, the chances of an ordinary weighing machine being able to detect a significant trend in weight over a reasonable period of time are negligible.

Weighing children does not help; weighing babies and weighing adolescents may help, because the rate of weight change is so much greater at these ages. But the clinical situation is usually so obvious that one needs eyes, not scales, to appreciate it.

Diagnosing the thin child

The principles of assessment are the same for thin children as for all other growth problems. The measurement of stature is useful and the measurement of growth velocity invaluable. A thin child who is growing at a normal rate (Fig. 7.1) presents much less of an anxiety than his slowly growing counterpart. The rate of growth preceding a consultation may be inferred from the present height in its relation to parental height, but it is no substitute for a

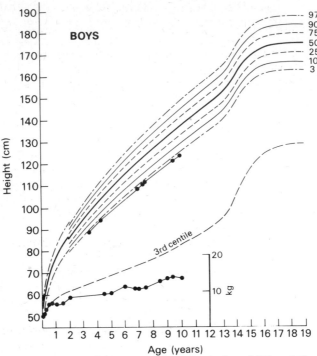

Fig. 7.1 Extremely poor weight gain during childhood (lower part of figure), in a boy who is growing normally in height and is otherwise well.

measurement of growth rate. In thin children, the diagnoses to seek are those in Table 7.1

The appearance of the lipodystrophic child is so striking that once seen it is never forgotten (Fig. 7.2). Such children may be tall as the result of increased growth hormone secretion, but although children with the syndromes of tall stature are also often thin, they do not resemble the lipodystrophic child. Low birthweight has been discussed before but it is worth mentioning here because the most invariable feature of the small-for-dates child is the difficult in feeding during infancy and early childhood. I do not know the explanation of this aspect of the problem, but in children referred to my hospital for thinness and/or feeding problems it is the commonest denominator.

Table 7.1 Causes of thinness in children.

Cause	Examples	Characteristics
Recognisable syndromes	Lipodystrophy (Fig. 7.2)	Easily visible muscle bundles
	Marfan syndrome (Fig. 5.2)	Tall stature and long limbs
	Low birthweight (Figs. 7.3 & 7.4)	Body asymmetry, characteristic facies and hands (Fig. 4.7)
Occult organic disease	Asthma	Short stature, cough, chest deformity
	Congenital heart disease	Short stature, cyanosis or murmur of left to right shunt
	Renal failure	Bone pain
	Diabetes	Glycosuria, polydipsia, enuresis
	Malignant disease	Hepatosplenomegaly
	Coeliac disease	Bone pain
	Cystic fibrosis	Short stature, delayed puberty
	Crohn's disease	Cough, abdominal pain
	Still's disease	Many painful episodes, intermittent fevers
	Cerebral palsy	Neurological signs
Psychological	Emotional deprivation	Short stature
	Anorexia nervosa Vomiting	Pubertal delay
Socioeconomic	Inadequate calories available	
	Unappetising calories provided	

Occasionally it is justifiable to make a diagnosis of 'Silver-Russell syndrome *sine* low birthweight' on the basis of the history of feeding difficulties associated with the characteristic facial appearance and body asymmetry (Figs. 7.3 & 7.4).

All serious illnesses cause thinness. The diseases highlighted in Table 7.1 are those which are not generally

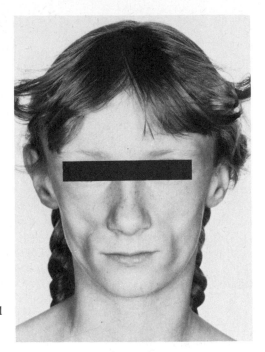

Fig. 7.2 Facial appearance of lipodystrophy.

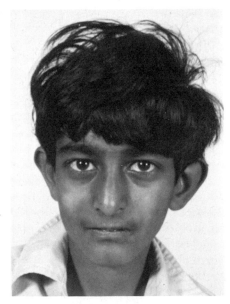

Fig. 7.3 The typical facies of low birthweight: note triangular face, asymmetry of the face and low set asymmetrical ears.

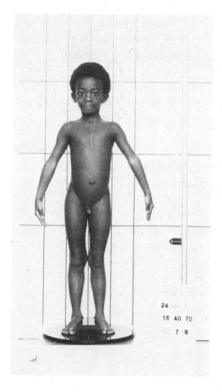

Fig. 7.4 Whole body asymmetry associated with low birthweight.

thought of in this context. Undertreated asthma is a case in point and is increasingly recognised as a cause of chronic ill–health in childhood. Gastrointestinal disease is obvious when it presents with bulky foul-smelling stools, but coeliac disease, cystic fibrosis, and Crohn's disease can be amazingly silent. Still's disease, too, presents in many guises. Congenital heart disease in general, and left-to-right shunts in particular, cause the expenditure of a large number of calories and need to be actively looked for. So do the less obvious neurological signs in cases of mild cerebral palsy who often seem to be thin. Diabetes, renal disease, and malignancies also need more than a passing thought in the thin child, especially if he is getting thinner. Psychological disorders are by far the toughest nut and by far the commonest cause of failure to thrive in childhood, whether or not they are recognised. The borderline

between normality and disorder in these cases is impossible
to draw and minor degrees of anorexia and major covert
vomiting have become amongst the most frequent causes
of pubertal delay (p.145).

In less affluent parts of the world the failure to provide
calories, alas, remains a major problem. In affluent
countries, calories are sometimes so unappetising that they
are foregone. Institutions rank high in this respect but
ethnic and cultural problems of nutrition are common in
the multiracial society of the United Kingdom.

It may be a matter of taste and thus of quantity: many
Indian children born in England prefer local food to their
own traditional cooking, which may offend the family. It
may be a matter of quality: the Indian diet is poor in iron
unless Indian vegetables are cooked in the traditional way.
When cabbage is substituted for beans, but the diet is
otherwise a vegetarian one, it becomes seriously iron
deficient.

Management of the thin child

A careful history and examination are essential.
Measurements of height and height velocity are
enormously helpful. Skinfold measurements provide the
best measure of body fatness and are particularly helpful
longitudinally, since the thin child who is growing
normally and not getting thinner needs no diagnosis. To
seek one is meddlesome, expensive, and also constitutes
bad medical practice. The reverse is also true and, once the
diagnosis has been made, treatment should be monitored
with the same tools. Once again, weight serves one badly,
as an illustrative case shows.

BS was eleven years of age when her anorexia nervosa
was diagnosed. Treatment was relatively satisfactory in
that 'target' weight was achieved over a period of three
months. The use of target weight may be dangerous in a
longstanding condition like this, because the patient could
see no good reason for disputing it. Consequently she
remained at 38 kg for 18 months, gradually becoming
thinner again as she grew. The introduction of a skinfold

thickness target brought a much more satisfactory result.

Can thinness be treated? Getting a child who is otherwise healthy to eat is difficult, frustrating, and unrewarding. It is usually also unavailing. Where there is a condition to be put right, the situation is quite different and treatment obviously depends on cause. Where the situation is normal, it is best to respect its normality and not to promote anxiety by seeking to change the status quo. The removal of parental anxiety will often be of major assistance in helping a child to eat more calories.

CHAPTER 8

Puberty

Physical signs of puberty, to which reference has already been made in Chapter 3, make their appearance in both sexes at about the same time. Fig. 8.1 shows the 50th centile timings for the acquisition of the various events of puberty, together with the range in 95% of cases. As can be seen, the major difference between the sexes lies in the timing of the peak of the adolescent growth spurt which comes early in the sequence of developments in girls and much later in boys.

There are no rules about pubertal development and it is impossible to forecast with any degree of accuracy the course of puberty in an individual. While the physical signs of puberty generally begin in girls with breast development and in boys with testicular enlargement, this is by no means always the case. Of 88 girls examined within three months after their pubic hair had begun to develop, 16% had no breast development. Conversely, of the 89 girls who were examined within three months after their breasts began to develop, 39% had pubic hair (Marshall & Tanner 1969). Out-of-step pubertal development is not unusual but occasionally extremes of variation do create clinical problems. Early events which are particularly overlooked are the secretion of apocrine sweat, which results from adrenal androgen secretion, and vaginal discharge, which results from oestradiol secretion. The amount of both may be sufficient to cause complaint. Although the sequence of events does vary in this way, the variation is much less than in the timing of the events both in onset and duration. Fifty per cent of girls progress from breast stage 2 to 5 in four years, but 3% may achieve this in as little as 18

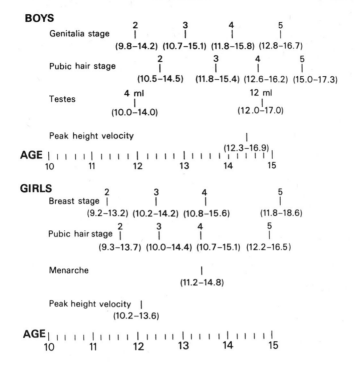

Fig. 8.1 The timing of events of puberty in boys and girls. The vertical lines indicate the 50th centile values and the ranges are shown in brackets.

months and 97% will have done so over nine years (Marshall 1977).

This enormous range may well result from the definition of breast stage 5 development but progression from pubic hair stage 2 to 5, which is easier to assess, takes 2.5 years in 50% of girls, 1.4 years in 3% and 3.1 years in 97%. Corresponding figures for development of male pubic hair are 1.6, 0.8 and 2.7 years. Again, the definition of male genitalia stage 5 is difficult but 50% of boys progress from genitalia stage 2 to 5 in 3.1 years, 3% do so in 1.9 years and 97% in 5.1 years. There seems no way to forecast the duration of puberty in individual instances and the timing of onset of puberty does not define the time that progression through the pubertal stages takes.

Timing of onset of puberty is presumed to be under some sort of genetic control, probably largely because so many children with late pubertal development have parents who give a history of similar late development. Without the knowledge of how many normal developers could give a similar history there are no data available to substantiate the genetic contribution to variations in the time of onset of puberty. Nor will there be until the children of subjects examined in one of the longitudinal growth studies reach puberty themselves.

Skeletal age is little better than chronological age for predicting the onset of normal puberty. In extreme advance or delay it may serve as a guide to the maturation of the whole growth process but Marshall (1974) has shown that only at menarche in normally maturing girls was skeletal age significantly less variable than chronological age for forecasting the events of puberty in either sex. Skeletal age remains a good guide to how much growth has passed and how much is to come, but it cannot predict the timing of the peak of the adolescent growth spurt.

The evidence that body composition relates to age and menarche (Frisch & Revelle 1971) is often mentioned in the context of amenorrhoea in anorexia nervosa. It has, however, been clearly shown that mean weights of menarche increase with increasing age and that, for given body weights, the proportion of girls starting to menstruate increases with age. Thus at all ages the variation of body weight at menarche is as large as that among non-menstruating girls (Billewicz et al 1976). Normal nutrition does not really seem to come into the pattern of pubertal development although the menstrual cycle is clearly subject to nutritional influences in pathological circumstances.

ENDOCRINE BACKGROUND

After the very active endocrine events of fetal life, the hypothalamo-pituitary-gonadal axis enters a period of relative quiescence in early childhood. Nevertheless, there is increasing evidence that some endocrine activity at a very low level is always present during early childhood and girls certainly show cyclical ovarian follicular development of low amplitude and long periodicity; the same may well also be true for boys.

The first generally accepted and well defined endocrine event of puberty is the increase in adrenal androgen production which takes place between the ages of five and eight years in both sexes (Parker *et al* 1978). This rise, which precedes the conventional changes of puberty (Ducharme *et al* 1976; Sizonenko *et al* 1976), may well be important in triggering the gonadotrophic events of puberty later. It is certainly so that children with congenitally absent adrenal glands fail to enter puberty normally due to an associated gonadotrophin deficiency (Hay *et al* 1981), while early puberty is a feature of uncontrolled adrenal androgen secretion in congenital adrenal hyperplasia (Klingensmith *et al* 1977). The control of adrenarche is not understood and is the object of much speculation at the moment. Certainly ACTH is extremely important in a permissive role, if not the primary stimulus to adrenal androgen secretion.

The role of the gonadotrophins in maintaining reproductive function in adult life is not in question. As Fig. 8.2 shows, there is a single hypothalamic gonadotrophin releasing hormone (GNRH) that is responsible for the stimulation of secretion of both LH and FSH by the pituitary gland. In the adult male, LH promotes secretion of testosterone from the Leydig cells and testosterone exerts a negative feed-back on pituitary release of LH. FSH causes maturation of the seminiferous tubules and spermatogenesis, and feedback is believed to be exerted by a hormone called inhibin. In the female, LH may be responsible for initiating steroidogenesis in the ovarian follicle, but FSH is certainly responsible for aromatisation and the release of oestradiol. During the maturation of the female hypothalamo–pituitary axis, the pituitary becomes sensitive to positive-feedback; thus increasing concentrations of oestradiol cause release of LH

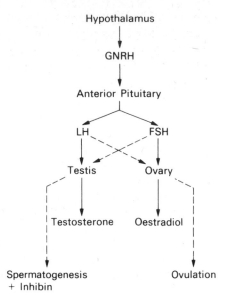

Fig. 8.2
The hypothalamo-
pituitary–gonadal
axis in adult life.

in mid-cycle when the female hypothalamo-pituitary axis is fully mature.

The way in which the prepubertal child develops this control system is far from understood. In prepuberty, gonadotrophin secretion is relatively quiescent, but nocturnal bursts of LH secretion herald the changes of puberty (Boyar *et al* 1972, Judd *et al* 1977). In both sexes, by the time puberty is complete, this sleep-enhanced secretion of gonadotrophins has been lost and during puberty it becomes less apparent as the general levels of gonadotrophins rise. During the prepubertal years, the pituitary remains responsive to stimulation with gonadotrophin-releasing hormone but quantitatively its responsiveness is age-dependent and qualitatively the FSH response is greater than that for LH which is the direct opposite of the situation after puberty (Dickerman *et al* 1976). It is possible that gonadotrophin release may be under tonic inhibition by another hormone and melatonin, the hormone of the pineal gland, has been proposed as a candidate for this role. Studies of melatonin have produced conflicting results in respect of puberty and at present its role as a puberty inhibitor remains conjectural.

On the basis of studies in normal individuals (Styne & Grumbach 1978) and on agonadal patients (Conte *et al* 1980) it has been suggested that the pituitary gland becomes progressively less sensitive to the inhibitory feedback of sex steroids as puberty advances. Thus gonadotrophin responsiveness to releasing hormone stimulation and gonadal sensitivity to gonadotrophic stimulation would both rise (Dickerman *et al* 1976, Winter *et al* 1972). As a model, the concept of the 'gonadostat' seems attractive but the data do not stand very close inspection and anyway fit much better for LH than for FSH. Our experience (C.G.D. Brook & M.A. Preece, unpublished observations) is that as puberty advances, the variation of responsiveness of gonadotrophin secretion to GNRH increases with age and stage of puberty, but that there is not an absolute progression of response. These findings are not at odds with the data of Styne and Grumbach (1978) but they alter their interpretation. At present, in the absence of large longitudinal studies, the concept of a lowering of the gonadostatic mechanism to enable the same concentration of GNRH to produce increasing amounts of gonadotrophin seems without secure foundation.

Since the demonstration that pulsatile administration of GNRH will produce normal menstural cycles (Leyendecker *et el* 1980), and puberty in infantile female monkeys (Knobil 1980), and since alteration in the strength and periodicity of stimulus alters gonadotrophin responsiveness, a maturation of GNRH secretion seems more probable than the gonadostat and fits the evidence available.

Cycling of gonadotrophins begins irregularly in females with a periodicity of 28-40 days (Winter & Faiman 1973). This is presumed to represent periodic maturation and regression of ovarian follicles, but, as the pituitary feedback system becomes less sensitive to the inhibition imposed by rising oestrogen levels, cycling develops into the regular pattern associated with menstruation. Menarche is determined by the presence of sufficient endometrial proliferation to allow the cyclic decline in oestrogen level to elicit the first menstrual bleed. Ovulation comes later because it is not until late in pubertal development that the hypothalamo–pituitary axis matures to the point where it responds to the positive-feedback of rising oestrogen levels with a surge of LH and FSH sufficient to induce ovulation. Irregular cycles are characteristic of early postmenarcheal development and these cycles may or may not be associated with ovulation. By the time the menstrual cycle becomes established, the feedback mechanism has matured sufficiently to be the reason why a single follicle ripens on each occasion. As FSH levels rise in the first half of the cycle, many ovarian follicles start to grow and oestrogen levels increase. The feedback mechanism ensures that FSH secretion is suppressed by this increase but as follicles generate receptor sites for FSH in relation to the oestrogen they produce, the more active follicles continue to mature in spite of an overall diminution of FSH secretion. Progressive elimination of the less active follicles allows the single most active one to persist and to ovulate in response to the gonadotrophin surge in mid-cycle.

Although this surge is dependent on positive oestrogen feedback, it must actually be occasioned by the slight fall in oestrogen production when the single most active follicle fails to be stimulated by the declining amounts of FSH available, since an oestrogen trough just precedes the LH peak. Whether or not progestogens play a part in the release of gonadotrophin in mid-cycle is not known but they do rise concomitantly with the LH increase, so they may have something to do with its cause (Nillius 1977).

In boys, FSH levels are greater in prepuberty and early puberty than values for LH and, as already indicated, FSH levels respond best to GNRH stimulation. It has been shown that after only 4-6 weeks of treatment with GNRH given in large doses subcutaneously eight hourly, the secretion of LH becomes greater than that of FSH to a single intravenous injection of GNRH (Mortimer 1977). Levels of FSH increase rapidly during the early phases of puberty and FSH is responsible for the initial increase in testicular size which is the first sign of puberty. It has been postulated that FSH induces sensitivity to LH (Franchi-mont & Roulier 1977) which induces the secretion of testosterone through the stimulation of the Leydig cells and leads to the development of the secondary sex characteristics. Judging from experience in using human chorionic gonadotrophin (LH) to induce puberty in hypogonadotrophic boys, LH must be responsible for an increase in testicular size of about 4-6 ml and FSH must be responsible for the remaining 15 ml to account for an adult testicular volume of 20-25 ml.

Although the sex steroids may exert some of their feed-back effects on GNRH secretion, they also exert moderating effects at pituitary level. There is substantial evidence for the presence of a substance produced by the testis that selectively inhibits secretion of FSH. This substance, inhibin, is produced during spermatogenesis but spermatogenesis requires the concurrent secretion of testosterone. Whether inhibin also effects LH secretion is debatable (Franchimont & Roulier 1977). The administra-tion of GNRH in constant amounts to hypogonadotrophic men and women suggests that pituitary feedback is the main modulator of gonadotrophin secretion.

At the same time as the relationships between the hypothalamus, pituitary, and gonads are becoming established, the hypothalamo–pituitary axis appears to become more active in the secretion of growth hormone. Growth hormone and sex steroids act synergistically in promoting the growth spurt in puberty (Aynsley-Green *et al* 1976, Tanner *et al* 1976). Growth hormone responsiveness to pharmacological stimuli is temporarily diminished in very late prepuberty but, when puberty begins, growth hormone levels rise and the pubertal growth spurt becomes quite normal.

It will be clear that the endocrine background to puberty is exceedingly complex and that we have as yet little or no information about the overall control of puberty. It becomes more complicated still when it is recognised that immuno-reactivity and bioactivity of hormones may be discrepant and that changes in bioactivity alone can explain much of what goes on (Lucky *et al* 1980). Puberty certainly seems to begin in the adrenal gland and then a series of carefully orchestrated changes in secretory patterns and feedback systems of the hormones of the hypothalamo–pituitary–gonadal axis brings about the physical changes.

Secondary sex characteristics

If the hypothalamo–pituitary–gonadal axis is in any way dysfunctional, failure of the development of secondary sex characteristics always occurs. In the male, testosterone is responsible for the growth of a penis, prostate, and seminal vesicles. Experience from male pseudo-hermaphrodites with steroid 5α-reductase deficiency suggests that testosterone itself, rather than dihydro-testosterone is the relevant hormone at this stage of development (Imperato-McGinley *et al* 1974). Whether males with steroid 5α-reductase deficiency can be fertile is not clear. If they are not, it may be because dihydrotestosterone is important for spermatogenesis.

The development of body hair has received rather little attention hitherto. Pubic hair appears concurrently with the growth of the penis, but axillary hair appears only when pubic hair is relatively well advanced. Facial hair in males appears later and hair elsewhere on the body (conspicuously on the chest) appears later still. This means that the hair follicles cannot just be unequally sensitive to differences in testosterone level, since maximal levels are reached long before body hair starts to appear in any amount. There must, therefore, be sequential maturation of testosterone receptors. Since it is now clear that the generation of receptors is at least as important as the secretion of hormones, the development of secondary sex hair deserves some study and might actually help in the management of hirsutism in females.

Breast development occurs in both sexes at puberty. The diameter of the areola, which is equal in both sexes before puberty, increases rapidly, doubling in diameter in boys and tripling in girls. Marked breast development occurs in a substantial proportion of boys during puberty and, in the large majority of these, it regresses spontaneously. In girls, breast development is a sensitive bioassay of oestradiol secretion but the observation of very early breast development in the presence of very low levels of oestradiol in some girls (premature thelarche) indicates again a difference in receptor sensitivity.

Given that testosterone can certainly be aromatised to oestradiol at tissue level in boys, it is curious why more boys do not develop breasts at puberty and why they regress. It is presumed that testosterone itself exerts an inhibiting activity on breast development, perhaps directly or perhaps by influencing aromatisation. Males given large doses of oestrogens, for example for carcinoma of the prostate, certainly develop adult breasts and after gonadectomy in the adult male, gynaecomastia becomes prominent unless testosterone replacement is adequate. Conversely excessive secretion of adrenal androgens in uncontrolled adrenal hyperplasia leads to very poor breast development in untreated adolescent girls.

There has been discussion about whether prolactin plays a part in the development of a pubertal breast. Prolactin levels change remarkably little during puberty on a cross-sectional basis (Franks & Brook 1976) but longitudinal studies suggest a small increment parallel to the increase in oestradiol (Apter *et al* 1978). Given that cosmetically normal breasts can be induced by oestradiol therapy alone in patients with hypopituitarism, it seems that prolactin probably plays little part in pubertal breast development.

Oestradiol is also responsible for promoting the growth of the uterus and vagina and for the development of the accessory vaginal exocrine glands. It is responsible for the thinning of the vaginal epithelium and the reduction in the glycogen content. The pH of the vaginal contents fairly accurately reflects oestradiol secretion and these changes in exocrine secretion are paralleled by the secretion of apocrine sweat.

The explanation of body hair in girls is difficult. In patients with gonadal dysgenesis, at least in those with the chromosomal abnormality of the Turner syndrome, pubic hair appears spontaneously in about 70% (Brook *et al* 1974). In such patients, a rapid increase in pubic hair occurs when oestradiol is administered to induce breast development. As the adrenal glands are the only source of androgens in the female, it has to be presumed that pubic and axillary hair in females is due to adrenal androgen secretion with oestrogens facilitating the receptor mechanism. In pathological conditions with excessive adrenal androgen secretion, women can become extremely hirsute. In some patients, the hirsutism can be reduced by the administration of dexamethasone, suggesting that it may be ACTH-driven, but a recent paper has indicated that cimetidine may occupy androgen receptor sites and could be useful in this respect (Vigersky *et al* 1980).

The adolescent growth spurt results from synergism between gonadal sex steroids and growth hormone, as long as other endocrine functions are normal. The sex steroids seem primarily responsible for the changes in the vertebral column and in the width of the shoulders and hips (Aynsley-Green *et al* 1976, Laron *et al* 1980, Tanner *et al* 1976). Growth of these parts occurs even when growth hormone is absent and is reduced by only about one-third. Conversely, growth of the legs is largely growth hormone development and a lack of sex steroids makes little difference to leg length. Thus an untreated patient with isolated growth hormone deficiency has a relatively long trunk with short limbs, while a gonadotrophin deficient patient has long legs and a short back. Excessive long-leggedness may result from long continued responsiveness to growth hormone in the absence of the epiphyseal maturing action of the sex steroids. Thus, in patients with diminished gonadal secretion, especially males, the legs may be longer than in normal males as well as long in proportion.

Enlargement of the larynx, cricothyroid cartilage, and laryngeal muscles, which leads to the breaking of the voice at about 13–14 years and the acquisition of an adult male voice by about 15–16 years is presumed to be due testosterone secretion. Nevertheless, it is said by singers that modification of the female voice continues over a longer period, which is difficult to understand. Striking other changes in body composition occur with increase in sex hormones. Lean body mass, skeletal mass, and body fat are approximately equal in young boys and girls but, by maturity, men have 1.5 times the lean body mass and 1.5 times the skeletal mass of woman, whereas women have twice as much body fat as men. As muscles increase in size, they also increase in strength and, as this increase is so much greater in boys than in girls, it is presumed to be a direct response of testosterone. The age-related rise in blood pressure cannot be simply testosterone-related, since the rise antedates testosterone secretion and starts around the time when adrenal androgens increase. Heart size and exercise tolerance are affected by these inter-relations but the latter is also affected by haemopoietic changes, since haemoglobin concentration in the blood modulated by erythropoietin is, at least to some extent, androgen-dependent, as evidenced by the effect of testosterone on patients with aplastic anaemia.

The reticuloendothelial system in general and the lymph glands and thymus in particular, are the only structures which do not show an adolescent spurt in growth; indeed the lymphatic tissue reaches a peak at around the age of 6-8 years and then actually decreases during adolescence. There seems to be no difference in the sexes in these changes but, given the complexity of the thymic humoral system which is now becoming evident, it would be unwise to deny that these changes may also have an endocrinological basis.

REFERENCES

APTER D., PAKARINEN A. & VIHKO R. (1978) Semen prolactin, FSH and LH during puberty in girls and boys. *Acta Paediatrica Scandinavica* **67**, 417-23.

AYNSLEY-GREEN A., ZACHMANN M. & PRADER A. (1976) Interrelation of the therapeutic effects of growth hormone and testosterone on growth in hypopituitarism. *Journal of Pediatrics* **89**, 992-9.

BILLEWICZ W.Z., FELLOWES H.M. & HYTTEN O.A. (1976) Comments on the cortical metabolic mass and the age of menarche. *Annals of Human Biology* **3**, 51-9.

BOYAR R., FINKELSTEIN J., ROFFWARG H. *et al* (1972) Synchronisation of augmented LH secretion with sleep during puberty. *New England Journal of Medicine* **287**, 582-6.

BROOK C.G.D., MÜRSET G., ZACHMANN M. *et al* (1974) Growth in children with 45 XO Turner syndrome. *Archives of Disease in Childhood* **39**, 789-95.

CONTE F. A., GRUMBACH M.M., KAPLAN S.L. (1980) Correlation of LHRH induced LH & FSH release from infancy to 19 years with the changing pattern of gonadotrophin secretion in gonadal patients: relation to the restraint of puberty. *Journal of Clinical Endocrinology and Metabolism* **50**, 163-8.

DICKERMAN Z., PRAGER-LEWIN R. & LARON Z. (1976) Response of plasma LH and FSH to synthetic LHRH in children at various pubertal stages. *American Journal of Diseases of Children* **130**, 634-8.

DUCHARME J.R., FOREST M.G., DE PERETTI E. *et al* (1976) Plasma adrenal and gonadal sex steroids in human pubertal development. *Journal of Clinical Endocrinology and Metabolism* **42**, 468-76.

FRANCHIMONT P. & ROULIER R. (1977) Gonadotophin secretion in male subjects. In Martini L. & Besser G.M. (eds.), *Clinical Neuroendocrinology,* pp. 197-212. Academic Press, New York.

FRANKS S. & BROOK C.G.D. (1976) Basal and stimulated prolactin levels in childhood. *Hormone Research* **7**, 65-76.

FRISCH R.E. & REVELLE R. (1971) Height and weight at menarche and a hypothesis of menarche. *Archives of Disease in Childhood* **46**, 695-701.

HAY I.D., SMAIL P.J. & FORSYTH C.C. (1981) Familial cytomegalic adreno-cortical hypoplasia: an X-linked syndrome of pubertal failure. *Archives of Disease in Childhood* **56**, 715-21.

IMPERATO-MCGINLEY J., GUERRERO L., GAUTIER T. *et al* (1974) Steroid 5α-reductase deficiency in man: an inherited form of male pseudohermaphroditism. *Science* (New York) **186**, 1213-5.

JUDD H.C., PARKER D.C. & YEN S.S.C. (1977) Sleep-wake patterns of LH and testosterone in prepubertal boys. *Journal of Clinical Endocrinology and Metabolism* **44**, 865-9.

KLINGENSMITH G.J., GARCIA S.C., JONES H.W. *et al* (1977) Glucocorticoid treatment of girls with congenital adrenal hyperplasia: effects on height, sexual maturation and fertility. *Journal of Pediatrics* **90**, 996-1004.

KNOBIL E. (1980) The neuroendocrine control of the menstrual cycle. *Recent Progress in Hormone Research* **36**, 53-88.

LARON Z., ROITMAN A. & KAULI R. (1980) Effect of human growth hormone therapy on head circumference in children with hypopituitarism. *Clinical Endocrinology* **10**, 393-9.

LEYENDECKER G., WILDT L. & HAUSMAN M. (1980) Pregnancies following chronic intermittent (pubertile) administration of GNRH by means of a portable pump. *Journal of Clinical Endocrinology & Metabolism* **51**, 1214-6.

LUCKY A.W., RICH B.H., ROSENFIELD R.L. *et al* (1980) LH bioactivity increases more than immunoreactivity during puberty. *Journal of Pediatrics* **97**, 205-13.

MARSHALL W.A. (1974) Interrelationships of skeletal maturation, sexual development and somatic growth in man. *Annals of Human Biology* **1**, 29-40.

MARSHALL W.A. (1977) *Human growth and its Disorders*. Academic Press, New York.

MARSHALL W.A. & TANNER J.M. (1969) Variation in the pattern of pubertal changes in girls. *Archives of Disease in Childhood* **44**, 291-303.

MORTIMER C.H. (1977) Gonadotrophin releasing hormone. In Martini L. & Besser G.M. (eds.) *Clinical Neuroendocrinology,* pp. 213-36. Academic Press, New York.

NILLIUS S.J. (1977) Normal gonadotrophin secretion in females. In Martini L & Besser G.M. (eds.) *Clinical Neuroendocrinology,* pp. 143-74. Academic Press, New York.

PARKER L.N., SACK J., FISHER D.A. & ODELL W.D. (1978) The adrenarche: prolactin, gonadotrophins, adrenal androgens and cortisol. *Journal of Clinical Endocrinology and Metabolism* **46**, 396-401.

SIZONENKO P.C., PAUNIER L. & CARMIGNAC D. (1976) Hormonal changes during puberty. *Hormone Research* **7**, 288-302.

STYNE D.M. & GRUMBACH M.M. (1978) Puberty in the male and female: its physiology and disorders. In S.S.C. Yen & R.B. Jaffe (eds.) *Reproductive Endocrinology,* pp. 189-240. W.B. Saunders, Philadelphia

TANNER J.M., WHITEHOUSE R.H., HUGHES P.C.R. *et al* (1976) Relative importance of growth hormone and sex steroids for the growth at puberty of trunk length, limb length and muscle width in growth hormone-deficient children. *Journal of Pediatrics* **89**, 1000-8.

VIGERSKY R.A., MEHLMAN I., GLASS A.R. *et al* (1980) Treatment of hirsute women with cimetidine. *New England Journal of Medicine* **303**, 1042.

WINTER J.S.D., TARASKA S., & FAIMAN C. (1972) The hormonal response to HCG in male children and adolescents. *Journal of Clinical Endocrinology and Metabolism* **34**, 348-53.

WINTER J.S.D. & FAIMAN C. (1973) The development of cyclic pituitary-gonadal function in adolescent females.*Journal of Clinical Endocrinology and Metabolism* **37**, 714-8.

CHAPTER 9

Early Puberty

Summary of diagnostic and therapy-orientated management of early puberty

1 Growth assessment. Is the pubertal development compatible in all respects?
2 If so, there is early activation of the normal pubertal mechanisms. Is there evidence of an intracranial lesion?
3 If not, seek an unusual source of sex steroids or cause of their secretion.
4 Is treatment of a primary condition indicated?
5 Should the physical signs of puberty be suppressed?

From the preceding account of the events of normal puberty it will be understood that it is difficult to absolutely define what is meant by early puberty. A reasonable working definition is that the acquisition of secondary sex characteristics before eight years in girls and nine years in boys constitutes an indication for concern. Early puberty is more common in girls than in boys, but the incidence of pathological causes is about the same in both sexes. Thus, in boys with early puberty, the chances of finding an abnormality are greater than in girls (Table 9.1) Cerebral causes of early puberty predominate in boys probably because pineal lesions are so seldom seen in girls.

PHYSIOLOGICAL EARLY PUBERTY

Isolated premature thelarche (breast development) is relatively common. It is almost always benign as long as it is truly unassociated with any other manifestation of

Table 9.1 Relative frequency of the causes of early puberty.

	Girls		Boys	
	n	%	n	%
Early activation of normal puberty				
Idiopathic	507	55	126	45
Cerebral causes	71	8	82	29
Ectopic source of gonadotrophins	4	<1	1	<1
Increased sex steroids				
Adrenal source				
virilising	272	29	69	25
feminising	8	1	1	1
Ovarian source	65	7	–	–
Testicular source	–	–	–	–
Total	927	100	279	100

Data from five published series (Reiter & Kulin 1972)

puberty, which includes an increase in growth velocity or the appearance of pubic hair. A careful physical examination, including examination of the optic fundi and, if possible, an assessment of visual fields, measurement of the skull circumference, and possibly a lateral X-ray of the skull are all that is required. It is probable that premature thelarche is an example of an extremely oestrogen-sensitive gland responding to the low levels of oestrogen which are present in very small girls. There may be long cycles of increasing and decreasing breast size as an illustration of this. In general, treatment and investigation of this condition should be resisted.

Tall stature has to be associated with early puberty if development is to end with the patient being a normal height because growth will come to an end early in this instance. Early puberty associated with tall stature is very likely to be physiological *as long as growth velocity is normal.* If the height velocity is increased before the time when the signs of puberty are first emerging, then the possibility of an abnormality becomes much greater, since this is not the usual pattern of events.

Overnutrition in the early months of life is associated with the acquisition of tall stature and proportionately advanced bone age. It has already been noted (p. 97) that the majority of infants gaining weight rapidly in the early months of life do not remain overweight or obese later. But the growth advance which has been imposed must remain, regardless of whether or not the children are very fat. It does not, however, seem to be associated with early pubertal maturation.

Laron *et al* (1978) studied 136 obese boys and 41 obese girls and confirmed that pubescent girls and boys with 'simple' obesity were taller and had a more advanced bone age than their controls. They could not, however, detect any significant difference between obese and control children as far as the appearance of secondary sex characteristics was concerned. These findings fit well with the point that has already been made that bone age is no better guide than chronological age to the onset of puberty. It is only when the whole process of maturation is achieved quickly that early puberty occurs. Bone age is only one aspect of maturation.

The management of patients with early puberty is really a question of how far to go in investigating individual cases and it is difficult to be very helpful in general. The condition is more often physiological in girls, so much so that the parent–offspring height correlation of girls who had had early puberty is no different from the normal, whereas in boys it is lost (Brook *et al* 1977), as one would expect of a pathological situation. The clinical approach necessitates bearing in mind the pathological conditions and being ready to pick up the slightest deviations in the course of puberty from the norm. Family history and socioeconomic circumstances, while they may contribute in general to the timing of onset of puberty, have no relevance in particular instances and should, for that reason, be disregarded in performing the relevant examination.

Table 9.2 Causes of pathological early puberty.

Intracranial causes
Space-occupying lesions anywhere, but especially of hypothalamus, third ventricle and pineal gland (usually in males)
Extracranial causes
Gonadal — ovarian tumours, testicular tumours
Adrenal — congenital adrenal hyperplasia, adrenal cortical neoplasm, Cushing syndrome
Ectopic gonadotrophin — hepatoblastoma
Miscellaneous causes with largely undefined mechanism
Mental retardation
Hypothyroidism
McCune-Albright syndrome
Drug ingestion

PATHOLOGICAL EARLY PUBERTY

In physiological early puberty the hypothalamo-pituitary-gonadal axis is activated early but the tempo of puberty is normal. It is as often the rapidity of the developing signs as the age of onset that requires explanation. The possibilities to be considered are shown in Table 9.2. In summary, they cover cerebral space-occupying lesions activating the hypothalamo-pituitary axis, some other reason for gonadotropic stimulation or an ectopic source of gonadotrophins leading to production of sex hormones. These may also be produced autonomously by the gonads, or may arise from extragonadal sources, particularly the adrenal glands. Drug ingestion must also be remembered.

The physical examination of the child with early puberty aims to cover these possibilities. With care and thought most of the pathological disorders can be diagnosed clinically. Examination should therefore include:

1 Measurement of height (and growth rate if possible).
2 Pubertal staging, including testicular size and evidence of oestrogenisation (labia, vagina, uterus).
3 Examination of the thyroid gland and thyroid status.
4 A search for skin pigmentation, depigmented areas and other signs characteristic of neurocutaneous dysplasias.
5 Abdominal palpation.
6 Examination of the central nervous system, including fundoscopy and charting of the visual fields.

One measurement of stature is only of limited help because children with physiological and pathological early puberty may both be tall. Growth rate may help to distinguish them because the former will have a growth rate compatible with their stage of puberty, whereas it may be discrepant in the latter. Normal stature should tend to raise the index of suspicion of pathology; short stature should do so still more.

Pubertal staging may help in drawing attention to a discrepant sequence of events: boys with stage 3 pubic hair ought not to have 2 ml testes and menstruating girls ought to have other signs of puberty. In the case of the former an alternate source of androgen production must be considered. It must also of course, be considered in a girl whose principal complaint is of the acquisition of pubic and other body hair. In these cases the adrenal gland is likely to be the suspect: there may be simple premature adrenarche, congenital adrenal hyperplasia, or neoplastic change of either benign or malignant nature. Cushing syndrome may also present in this way.

In females it is especially important to examine the genital area. Heller *et al* (1978) have shown that, of 51 girls whose evidence of early puberty was vaginal bleeding, no less than six had genital tumours and a further eight had local causes of bleeding.

Examination of the thyroid gland is important, since hypothyroidism is one of the commoner causes of early puberty. In primary hypothyroidism, which is most commonly autoimmune in origin and consequently is more often found in girls, TSH levels rise in response to TRH stimulation. TRH is a powerful and reliable stimulator of prolactin secretion and also causes release of FSH (Barnes *et al* 1978). This leads to ovarian production of oestradiol and breast enlargement and the patient does not have to be obviously hypothyroid for this mechanism to operate. A failing thyroid gland may be supported by excessive TRH drive and able thereby to maintain a euthyroid state and yet be the cause of early puberty. Hypothyroidism in males is associated with increased testicular size, presumably by the same mechanism (Laron *et al* 1970).

In neurofibromatosis, café-au-lait spots are characteristic features and are usually not easily confused with the darker, jagged-edged lesions seen with polyostotic fibrous dysplasia of bone in the McCune–Albright syndrome. In neurofibromatosis, intracranial involvement can lead to early and also late puberty. In McCune-Albright syndrome there seems to be autonomous functioning of a number of endocrine glands and early puberty is a characteristic association. It is probably not of hypothalamic origin as was previously supposed. Tuberous sclerosis is another neurocutaneous disorder which can be associated with early puberty when there is intracranial involvement and a search should be made for adenoma sebaceum and shagreen patches. Mental retardation is often associated with early puberty, irrespective of the aetiology of the mental retardation. Obviously the neurocutaneous dysplasias do sometimes provide a link.

By abdominal palpation it is hoped to detect ectopic sources of hormone production. Hepatoblastoma may secrete human chorionic gonadotrophin or LH, either of which may cause sex hormone production. Ovarian tumours may secrete oestrogen autonomously and testicular tumours do also occur, but they are the least common cause of early puberty. Heller *et al* (1978) could find no cases of ovarian tumours in 51 girls presenting with vaginal bleeding.

Careful examination of the central nervous system, fundoscopy and charting of the visual fields cannot be over-emphasised. Any intracranial lesion can present with early puberty — some do so particularly. Tumours which destroy the pineal gland occur principally in males, but hypothalamic lesions (hamartoma, congenital malformations, and other tumours) occur in both sexes. Intracranial lesions near the third ventricle, especially optic nerve gliomas, often precipitate early activity of the hypothalamo–pituitary axis, as may any cause of internal hydrocephalus. Cerebral and meningocerebral infections (encephalitis, meningitis, toxoplasmosis) may also do so, as may some of the degenerative disorders. The neurocutaneous dysplasias have already been mentioned, but the slightest doubt about the normality of the central nervous system must be followed up, especially now that it is possible to do so with non-invasive techniques of investigation (computerised axial tomography or computer emission tomography). It should be stressed here that the finding of an abnormality does not necessarily constitute an indication for treatment (see below).

Management

Early puberty is a cause of social and psychological disturbance and, apart from dealing with the obvious pathological situations (e.g. treating hydrocephalus or hypothyroidism), the question of whether or not it requires treatment is more a social than a medical matter. If a patient does not mind being unusually precocious (which is rare) there is no medical advantage to be gained by arresting pubertal development.

The major long-term physical disadvantage of early puberty is the short stature which results from reduction of the time of prepubertal growth and the fusion of the epiphyses which is the inevitable consequence of sex steroid secretion. It has already been emphasised that skeletal maturity plays very little part in determining the onset of puberty, but sex steroids make a major contribution to advancing bone age. Unfortunately, therefore, by the time a diagnosis of early puberty has been made, skeletal maturity is often already well advanced and the growth that has not occurred to keep the advance proportionate cannot be, and cannot be expected to be, recovered, regardless of what happens later. The situation for growth is as bad at the time of diagnosis as it will ever become; consequently, treatment of the clinical symptoms of early puberty with anti-gonadotrophin agents, even if they have an anti-androgenic effect, will make no difference to the situation (Werder *et al* 1974).

Two anti-gonadotrophic drugs are available for the treatment of the clinical effects of puberty: cyproterone acetate and danazol. Both are extremely effective in suppressing signs of pubertal development in both sexes and especially at stopping menstruation, which is often the most distressing event to the early-maturing girl. Cyproterone suppresses the hypothalamo-pituitary-adrenal axis (Hormone Research 1977, Girard *et al* 1978, Savage & Swift 1981) so that subjects taking this drug should carry a steroid card. No clinical effects have been found to result from this suppression. Danazol is probably free of this problem (Smith & Harris 1979). Medroxyprogesterone and chlormadinone acetate have been used previously to suppress menstruation: neither was as successful as the newer anti-gonadotrophin agents.

A possible future line for treatment may evolve from the waning of gonadotrophin response to the releasing hormone which was noted when large doses of gonadotrophin releasing hormone were given in attempt to induce delayed puberty (Brook & Dombey 1979). A highly potent long-acting analogue of gonadotrophin releasing hormone is available and has been used clinically as an oral contraceptive. It may find a use in the suppression of signs of early puberty (Comite *et al* 1982) but it is certainly too early generally to recommend this treatment at the time of writing.

Where extracranial causes of precocious puberty are discovered, treatment of the primary condition should, of course, be instituted where possible. With intracranial causes the matter is not straightforward, because neurosurgical procedures may cause more problems than they solve. Indeed, it is generally true in paediatrics to say that neurosurgery never improves the endocrine situation

— Cushing syndrome, gigantism and hyperprolactinaemia being possible exceptions to this statement. Malignant neoplasms, of course, require treatment in their own right, but most of the intracranial neoplasms which present with early puberty are very slow growing and removal of them has, from the endocrinological point of view, the hazard of preventing pubertal development as well as causing other endocrine effects. In the present state of knowledge, induction of puberty is very unsatisfactory, worse now than attempts at suppressing the effects of early puberty, even though other endocrine problems can be managed. For this reason, intracranial intervention should be done solely on neurosurgical grounds (hydrocephalus, field defect, etc.) and never on endocrinological ones. Where medical management of early puberty has been decided, doses of the chosen medication should be based on surface area and increased as the child grows. Medication should be discontinued when the child's peers are beginning to enter an equivalent stage of pubertal development.

REFERENCES

BARNES N.D., JONES J. & GRANT D.B (1978) TRH releases FSH in children: an explanation for the elevated FSH levels in juvenile hypothyroidism. *Pediatric Research* **12**, 155.

BROOK C.G.D. & DOMBEY S. (1979) Induction of puberty: longterm treatment with high dose LHRH. *Clinical Endocrinology* **11**, 81-7.

BROOK C.G.D., GASER T., WERDER E.A. *et al* (1977) Height correlations between parents and mature offspring in normal subjects and in subjects with Turner's, Klinefelter's and other syndromes. *Annals of Human Biology* **4**, 17-22.

COMITE F., CUTLER G.B., RIVIER J. *et al* (1981) Short-term treatment of idiopathic precocious puberty with a long-acting analogue of luteinizing hormone — releasing hormone. *New England Journal of Medicine* **305**, 1546-50.

GIRARD J. BAUMANN J.B., BUHLER V. *et al* (1978) Cyproterone acetate & ACTH-adrenal function. *Journal of Clinical Endocrinology and Metabolism* **47**, 581-6.

HELLER M.E., SAVAGE M.O. & DEWHURST J. (1978) Vaginal bleeding in childhood: a review of 51 patients. *British Journal of Obstetrics and Gynaecology* **85**, 721-5.

HORMONE RESEARCH (1977) Proceedings of a discussion, Berlin (1977) Treatment of idiopathic precocious puberty with cyproterone acetate. *Hormone Research* **9**, 301-12.

LARON Z., KARP M. & DOLBERG L. (1970) Juvenile hypothyroidism with testicular enlargement. *Acta Paediatrica Scandinavica* **59**, 317-22.

LARON Z. BEN DAM I., SHREM M. *et al* (1978) Puberty in simple obese boys and girls. In Cacciari E., Laron Z. & Raiti S. (eds.) *Obesity in Childhood,* Academic Press, New York.

REITER E.D. & KULIN H.E. (1972). Sexual maturation in the female — normal development and precocious puberty. *Pediatric Clinics of North America* **19,** 581.

SAVAGE D.C.L. & SWIFT P.G.F. (1981) Effect of cyproterone acetate on adrenocortical function in children with precocious puberty. *Archives of Disease in Childhood* **56,** 218-22.

SMITH C.S. & HARRIS F. (1979) Role of danazol in the management of precocious puberty. *Postgraduate Medical Journal* **55** (Suppl. 5) 81-6.

WERDER E.A., MÜRSET G., ZACHMANN M. *et al* (1974) Treatment of precocious puberty with cyproterone acetate. *Pediatric Research* **8,** 248-54.

CHAPTER 10

Late Puberty

Summary of diagnostic and therapy-orientated management of late puberty

1 Growth assessment. Is the patient tall or small in relation to pubertal development? Are there any signs of pubertal development and if so are they consistent with each other.

2 If the patient has height and pubertal development consonant for each other, physiological late puberty is probably present. Does it require therapy?

3 If the patient is tall, consider gonadotrophin deficiency or possibly Klinefelter syndrome in a boy.

4 If the patient is small, consider panhypopituitarism or possibly Turner syndrome in a girl.

5 If pubertal signs are not consistent (e.g. breast development without pubic hair and amenorrhea), the diagnosis should be considered without the context of normal pubertal endocrinology.

Of all the presenting symptoms of problems in growth, late puberty is probably the commonest. The reason for this was encapsulated in Fig. 8.1 (p.121) which showed the timing and sequence of events in male and female puberty. It indicated that 97% of boys and girls had shown evidence of pubertal development by the age of about 14 years. This still leaves about 3% of children who will not have done so and the majority of these will be quite normal. Once again, it is the distinction between the physiological and the pathological situations which is important.

PHYSIOLOGICAL LATE PUBERTY

When late puberty is accompanied by short stature and retarded bone age, the likelihood is that it is all part of growth delay, to which reference has been made previously (p. 66). There is often a family history of growth delay and late puberty, but this is not invariable and is by no means a *sine qua non* of making this diagnosis. The condition presents more commonly in boys than in girls; this may be partly because the early changes of puberty are easier to spot in girls than in boys, but probably represents a true sex difference, just as girls tend more often to have physiological early puberty. Again, the sex incidence of central pathology is similar (Table 10.1).

The main differential diagnoses to be considered in a patient with presumed physiological delay, who is necessarily short, are gonadotrophin deficiency associated with partial growth hormone deficiency (partial, because total growth hormone deficiency would have led to consideration of the short stature of itself, rather than of pubertal delay) and, in females, forms of gonadal dysgenesis.

Table 10.1 Relative frequency of the causes of late puberty.

	Girls		Boys	
	n	%	n	%
Idiopathic delay	12	16	63	50
Hypothalamo–pituitary problems	27	36	43	34
isolated gonadotrophin deficiency	4	5	12	9
multiple hormone deficiencies	9	12	19	16
space-occupying lesions	14	19	12	9
Gonadal problems	30	40	8	6
Emotional and systemic disorders	5	8	12	10
Totals	74	100	126	100

Data from Chaussain (1981).

In theory, measurements of growth velocity should distinguish the pathological conditions, but in practice it can be very difficult, unless there have been measurements of height earlier in childhood. The reason for this lies in the gradual deceleration of growth which precedes the onset of the adolescent growth spurt. Unfortunately, there is no study which quantifies velocity centiles in late prepuberty and the best one can do is to continue by eye, the downward trend of prepubertal velocity to extrapolate what is a normal velocity for a prepubertal 17-year-old. With hindsight, it is all very easy; in prospect it is seldom so plain.

Fig. 10.1 shows the distance chart of a girl with physiological growth delay and late puberty. She presented at age eleven with short stature (125 cm) and no evidence of pubertal development. Her bone age was eight years,

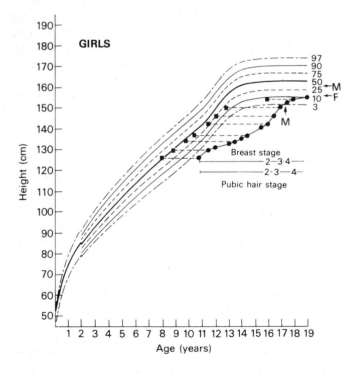

Fig. 10.1 Physiological late puberty in a girl.

which meant that at the time of presentation 80% of her growth had already occurred, giving her a height prediction of 156 cm, which lies, as can be seen, well within the centiles for her parental height. Almost any diagnosis could fit this situation. Turner syndrome, or Turner mosaicism, would fit well — and there do not have to be obvious physical signs. Hypothyroidism, Cushing syndrome, partial growth hormone deficiency, craniopharyngioma or other space-occupying lesions affecting the hypothalamo–pituitary axis, pseudohypo-parathyroidism, coeliac disease, anorexia nervosa, etc. — all would fit equally. There may be other signs of these conditions, but they are not invariable. Isolated gonadotrophin deficiency and primary gonadal failure are, by comparison, relatively unlikely diagnoses because of the short stature.

In this case, as is usual in practice, there were no previous measurements of height which would have helped decide on grounds of height velocity whether or not there was a problem. Consequently, a wait-and-see policy is the only alternative to time-consuming, expensive, and sometimes painful investigation. With the least prompting I would request a skull radiograph, a serum thyroxin estimation, and a karyotype, but much more information will accrue from a six month velocity. Fig. 10.1 shows the velocity and subsequent ones — and depressingly low they became, so that by 14 years the girl was growing very slow-ly indeed. Investigation at this stage may compound the problem, because such slow growth is either associated with or the cause of the hypothalamo-pituitary axis becom-ing relatively unresponsive to the usual pharmacological stimuli of growth hormone secretion. Since it recovers completely when puberty begins, this is presumed to be the result and not the cause of the whole situation, unless perhaps an as yet undefined decrease in growth hormone secretion is a key to the prepubertal deceleration of height velocity.

Slow though they may be, however, all these velocities lie on a projection of the decelerating prepubertal 50th height velocity centile and this is why the likelihood of any of the disorders mentioned as being the cause of the problem was small. But it is easy to say this with hindsight when one can see that pubertal signs began to develop at 16 years, the height spurt occurred in proper sequence, menarche occurred at 17 years (when the bone age had reached exactly 13 years and when the growth spurt was beginning to slow down) and growth ceased at the predicted height. Fortunately, cases as extreme as this are relatively uncommon and often in males, who are more usually involved, one can detect early enlargement of the testes and so have no lingering doubts that all may not be well.

Table 10.2   Causes of pathologically delayed puberty.

Hypothalamic   Gonadotrophin-releasing hormone deficiency either isolated or as part of a multiple hormone deficiency

Emotional causes, e.g. anorexia nervosa
Systemic illness
Associated with other endocrine disorders, e.g. hypothyroidism, congenital adrenal hypoplasia
Space-occupying lesions causing a direct effect
Postoperative
Idiopathic

Pituitary   Gonadotrophin deficiency either isolated or as part of a multiple hormone deficiency

Space-occupying lesion having a direct effect, including prolactinomas
Postoperative
Idiopathic (including Kallmann syndrome)

Gonadal   Sex steroid deficiency

Anorchia or hypoplastic testes
Ovarian dysgenesis
Enzyme defects, e.g. 20, 22 desmolase, 3β-hydroxysteroid dehydrogenase, 17α-hydroxylase, 17, 20 desmolase, 17α-reductase, aromatase deficiencies

PATHOLOGICAL LATE PUBERTY

The causes of pathologically late puberty are shown in Table 10.2. About 10% of children going late into puberty have a non-endocrine cause and a low growth velocity should draw attention to an emotional or systemic illness causing delayed puberty. Blunted gonadotrophin responsiveness is an almost invariable feature of anorexia nervosa; it is also commonly seen in all cases of undernutrition and degrees of this in both boys and girls may be difficult to spot without measuring skinfold thicknesses. Stature may have been adequate before pubertal development was expected, so these patients are not necessarily short. On the other hand, gastrointestinal disorders (Crohn's disease, ulcerative colitis, and coeliac disease), respiratory problems (undertreated asthma), and poorly treated diabetes mellitus are all relevant medical conditions presenting with short stature as well as pubertal delay.

Deficiencies of hypothalamo–pituitary hormones account for about one-third of children of both sexes who fail to enter puberty at the right time. In the case of isolated gonadotrophin deficiency (or deficiency of the releasing hormone) the patients are of normal stature, whereas in multiple hormone deficiencies, which usually include growth hormone, they will either be short or will be growing inadequately. In idiopathic cases, the deficiencies are generally of long standing, so short stature is prominent; in cases of space-occupying lesions, zero or near zero growth velocity is a common feature.

Hyperprolactinaemia has recently become recognised as a cause of late puberty (Koenig *et al* 1977). Generally it is associated with radiographic changes caused by the extension of the intrasellar prolactinoma but micro-adenomata causing hyperprolactinaemia are probably more common than has previously been recognised.

Some 40% of girls and 5% of boys entering puberty late do so as result of a gonadal problem. In the case of boys, testes must have been present to allow male sexual differentation, but they certainly can disappear later and may have been damaged by previous surgical intervention. Alternatively, they may be unresponsive to pituitary signals, even though they are actually palpable. In both these situations, gonadotrophin levels will be raised and this is the classical finding in males with Klinefelter syndrome — of which tall stature for parents due to long legs is characteristic. Patients with bilateral cryptorchidism not infrequently have hypogonadotrophic hypogonadism in which case gonadotrophin levels are not raised. Such patients presenting at any age should be investigated to exclude endocrinological abnormality: this does not, of course, apply to unilateral undescent of the testes.

In girls gonadal dysgenesis may be congenital or acquired, the former is much more frequent but chemotherapy or radiotherapy for cancer may be expected to cause problems. In congenital instances, Turner syndrome and its variants are prominent but not all patients have the typical dysmorphic features. Of those that do, and short stature is the least variable feature, 50% have a karyotype 45XO and a further 40% have some form of sex chromosomal mosaicism. Of the remaining 10%, about half have a normal female karyotype and half a Y chromosome or chromosomal fragment. This latter group is important because of the greatly increased chance of malignant change in the dysgenetic gonads of such patients. Since there may be no dysmorphic features at all, there is an indication for chromosome analysis in all patients being investigated for pathologically delayed puberty. The hallmark of patients with a gonadal cause is raised basal levels of gonadotrophins.

Enzyme defects causing delayed puberty are not common and should have been anticipated by events earlier in childhood, but deficiencies of all the enzymes in the pathways of sex steroid biosynthesis have been described. Their characterisation is not part of this text.

Investigation of pathologically delayed puberty

As will already be clear, the physical examination and growth record of patients go a long way in making a diagnosis. Signs of adrenarche (pubic and axillary hair) should be sought; they are usually only completely absent in pituitary gonadotrophin deficiency. A karyotype is needed if there is any suggestion that a male patient has long legs or tall stature, gynaecomastia, small genitalia, or a poor school performance, as these are all signs of Klinefelter syndrome or of similar chromosomal abnormalities. In females, a karyotype is mandatory. The estimation of basal levels of LH and FSH helps to decide whether the problem is gonadal or otherwise. Hypergonadotrophic hypogonadism in females may require laparoscopy to define the state of the ovaries and the relevance of the karyotype has already been stressed.

A defective sense of smell in the patient or his relatives suggest gonadotrophin deficiency (Kallmann syndrome) and injection of gonadotrophin-releasing hormone will fail to release gonadotrophins. Sense of smell may, however, be intact in gonadotrophin deficiency. In the presence of testes of prepubertal size and no other signs of puberty, an LHRH test is certainly the next one to perform and this recommendation also applies to females. In the presence of short stature, the LHRH test should be combined with a complete assessment of hypothalamo-pituitary function, which includes measurements of basal and stimulated levels of prolactin.

The aim of these tests is to identify hypothalamic and pituitary causes of delayed puberty. Often it is difficult to be sure whether the hypothalamus or pituitary is primarily defective. Gonadotrophin-releasing hormone deficiency acquired prenatally probably causes failure of development of pituitary gonadotrophs. But repeated stimulation with gonadotrophin-releasing hormone can promote pituitary gonadotrophin secretion in some cases, suggesting that gonadotrophs may have developed but be functionally inactive as a result of continuing releasing hormone deficiency. The results of gonadotrophin-releasing hormone tests divide into responders and non-responders, with a few cases where the response is detectable but smaller than normal. In the latter instances repeated stimulation with releasing hormone may induce responsiveness, inferring releasing hormone deficiency.

Administration of gonadotrophins will cause release of sex steroids from the gonads in both sexes. The testosterone response of testes stimulated by human chorionic gonadotrophin (LH) is much better quantified (Zachmann 1972) than the ovarian response to follicle stimulating hormone (FSH) because, if ovaries are present, they respond to FSH and if they are not, FSH levels are high. Testicular development requires gonadotrophic stimulation and in true hypogonadotrophic hypo-gonadism, which is characterised by low basal levels of gonadotrophins and absent gonadotrophin response to gonadotrophin-releasing hormone stimulation, LH receptors in the testes seem to be lacking which leads to poor or absent testosterone response to LH. If gonadotrophins are absent in women, their administration usually stimulates the ovary and induction of ovulation is much more successful than induction of spermatogenesis.

Investigation of delayed puberty therefore comprises:

1 Physical examination, including measurement of stature.
2 Assessment of pubertal status.
3 Establishment of growth velocity.
4 Testing visual fields.
5 Testing sense of smell.
6 Skull radiograph — ? proceed to other neuro-radiological investigations.
7 Assessment of skeletal maturity.
8 Karyotype.
9 Estimation of basal levels of prolactin.
10 Estimation of basal gonadotrophin levels and their response to gonadotrophin-releasing hormone stimulation.
11 Estimation of basal sex steroid levels and their response to appropriate gonadotrophic stimulation.
12 Assessment of hypothalamo–pituitary function, where short stature is an otherwise unexplained feature.

Management of treatment

Management in the majority of instances first involves

waiting for some weeks or months. Sometimes the psychological disadvantages of being very short or very delayed or both, are sufficient to warrant treatment. Sex steroids can be used to induce puberty but such steroids are given at the potential risk of decreasing ultimate height. If the patient is not short or has a normal growth prediction, this may be of secondary importance, but in practice the child is normally short and the growth prediction barely adequate, so that room for manoeuvre is restricted. Anabolic steroids in small doses may be helpful in bringing forward the growth spurt that would anyway occur later. They do not and cannot be expected to increase final height achieved but they may achieve it earlier which may be desirable. At the time of writing, the indication and consequences of their use are not sufficiently quantified to make a general recommendation and this is an area when referral to a specialist growth assessment centre may be helpful.

Where a definite cause of pathologically delayed puberty has been delineated, treatment should be aimed at correcting it and correcting it at the appropriate time to keep development in line with the patient's peers. Where an endocrine cause is found, replacement therapy is required. The administration of gonadotrophin-releasing hormone in the long-term has been rather disappointing (Brook & Dombey 1979). Although it has been possible to initiate the changes of puberty, it has been very difficult to maintain biochemical responsiveness to gonadotrophin-releasing hormone. This is probably a dose phenomenon and is under investigation since gonadotrophin-releasing hormone replacement in suitable cases potentially offers the best prospects for fertility. Both pulsatile administration and infrequent intranasal insufflation of the releasing hormone are under review.

When gonadotrophins are absent, administration of human chorionic gonadotrophin on a chronic basis enables sufficient testosterone to be secreted by the testes to bring about the physical changes of puberty. It is probable that such treatment should not be unduly prolonged because there is a possibility of tubular damage following long-term or high dose administration of hCG. FSH may be added later to induce spermatogenesis.

In girls, follicle stimulating hormone should not be used chronically to induce puberty. This treatment causes dysfunctional uterine bleeding and carries the risk of rupturing an ovarian cyst. Further, while spermatogenesis is an active process requiring the testis to be producing testosterone, oogenesis took place during the period of embryogenesis and ovulation can be induced later after puberty has been established.

In the situation where primary gonadal failure is the cause of late development or when other methods of inducing puberty are not to be used or are not successful, sex steroids can be administered by themselves. Two rules should be followed: first, initial doses should be very small (as they are in normal puberty), otherwise the physical and psychological consequences can be very distressing. Secondly, the timetable of normal puberty should be followed which means a duration of therapy between two and three years to achieve complete sexual development. If treatment were begun at an appropriate age, this would not be a problem. Unfortunately, it often seems to be excessively delayed in which case a rushed job is accomplished which leaves the patient often shorter than he or she might have been and, more importantly, in an emotional whirl.

In boys, therefore, testosterone should be given in small doses, either by depot injections of long acting testosterone esters at gradually reducing intervals (starting with 100 mg at six weekly intervals and reducing to 250 mg thrice weekly) or by one of the newer oral preparations. Unfortunately there are none of these on the market in small enough doses at present to start treatment but they may appear. For maintenance therapy, oral replacement is very suitable.

Ethinyl oestradiol should be commenced in very small doses 5–10 µg daily and should probably be given continuously in the first instance. This should not continue for too long since breakthrough bleeding will occur and there may be a very small risk of carcinogenesis. After about six months, therefore, or if dysfunctional uterine bleeding were to occur before, a five day course of progestogen (e.g. norethisterone acetate 5 mg daily) should be given by cessation of therapy for a week to allow a withdrawal bleed. The oestrogen should then be combined with a progestogen and given cyclically; an ultra-low dose oral contraceptive pill may be very suitable. The dose of ethinyl oestradiol should not exceed 20 µg for at least another six months, when it may be increased to 30 µg taken cyclically. There is rarely a need to use larger doses of oestrogen than this to get cosmetically normal pubertal development in girls and larger doses cause undesirable side-effects and unnecessary hazards. Since sex steroids cannot induce fertility, they must be regarded as cosmetic at best.

Amenorrhoea

Strictly, this is not a disorder of growth and development within the context of this chapter, since in the majority of instances it presupposes that other pubertal signs have developed quite normally. When they have failed to do so, the investigation is along the lines already indicated. In true primary amenorrhoea the cause has to be due either to an obstruction to menstrual flow or to the absence of a uterus. The latter situation, primary androgen insensitivity (testicular feminisation), is probably the most likely diagnosis and in this situation (or indeed in any girls with a 'Y' chromosome present) gonadectomy is required, certainly after puberty, if not before. If gonadectomy has been carried out before puberty, the use of conjugated oestrogens in a girl without a uterus is recommended for the induction of puberty. Secondary amenorrhoea is quite a different condition, most frequently due to psychological causes but possibly of organic origin, and the reader is referred to the article by Jacobs *et al* (1975).

Cryptorchid testes

These are not really part of pubertal development either, but they do come within the compass of problems of growth and development. The normal testis descends towards the end of pregnancy as a result of gonadotrophin-induced secretion of testosterone acting on the gubernaculum. There can, therefore, be only three reasons for a testis failing to descend. Gonadotrophins may not be produced, the testis may not produce testosterone, or it may not be anatomically possible for it to descend. In unilateral cases, the last is much the most probable: in bilateral instances it is less likely.

A testis which fails to descend to the scrotum before the age of eight years is most unlikely to be functionally adequate in spermatogenesis. This is probably because such a testes is atrophic (which is the reason it has not descended) but, in case the position is critical to testicular development, every attempt should be made to ensure that testes are in the scrotum well before the age of school entry. If they are simply retractile, there is no cause of concern: a retractile testis can be manipulated into the scrotum and will invariably descend under the influence of its own testosterone secretion at puberty. If necessary this can be tested by administering human chorionic gonadotrophin (say 3000 IU) over a week or two and observing descent. If testes are ectopic, they must be placed in the scrotum but the higher they lie, the more likely is a primary abnormality of testicular development (Dougall *et al* 1974). Nevertheless, as long as the abnormality is unilateral, it is of not great consequence.

In bilateral true cryptorchidism the situation is potentially more serious and all boys with this condition should undergo LHRH and hCG stimulation tests before surgery. A substantial number will have hypogonadotrophic hypogonadism and these patients can be saved the anxiety of waiting for a puberty that will not occur. Unfortunately, there are still no data adequate to determine the incidence of malignant change in undescended testes, but there seems little doubt that it is extremely low in non-functioning testicular tissue. Accordingly, it is probably not worth advising on difficult exploration and often fruitless operation for a boy with bilateral cryptorchidism and no biochemical responsiveness to human chorionic gonadotrophin. Where functional testicular tissue is ectopic, it should be removed.

REFERENCES

BROOK C.G.D. & DOMBEY S. (1979) Induction of puberty: long term treatment with high-dose LHRH. *Clinical Endocrinology* 11, 81-87.

CHAUSSAIN, J.L. (1981) Late Puberty. In C.G.D. Brook (ed.) *Clinical Paediatric Endocrinology,* Blackwell Scientific Publication Oxford.

DOUGALL A.J., MACLEAN N. & WILKINSON A.W. (1974) Histology of the maldescended testis at operation. *Lancet* 1, 771-4.

JACOBS H.S., HULL M.G.R. MURRAY M.A.F. & FRANKS S. (1975) Therapy orientated diagnosis of secondary amenorrhoea *Hormone Research,* 6 268-87.

KOENIG, M.P. ZUPPINGER K. & LEICHTI B. (1977) Hyperprolactinaemia as a cause of delayed puberty. Successful treatment with Bromocryptine. *Journal of Clinical Endocrinology and Metabolism,* 45, 825—6.

ZACHMANN M. (1972) The evaluation of testicular endocrine function before and in puberty. *Acta Endocrinologica,* 70 (suppl.) 164.

Index

Abdominal palpation, in early
    puberty   139
ACTH treatment, growth and
    skeletal maturity,
    effects   68-9
Adolescence   see Puberty
Adrenal androgen,
    secretion   120, 123,
    129, 130
Adrenal disease, and tall
    child   91
Adrenal hyperplasia   129, 138
Adrenarche   26, 151
    premature   138
    see also Puberty
Amenorrhoea   113, 122, 155
Anabolic steroids, use in
    puberty induction   153
    Turner syndrome   64-5
Anorexia nervosa   21, 113, 115,
    118-19, 149
Apocrine sweat, secretion, in
    early puberty   120
Arachnodactyly, congenital
    contractural   86
Arm circumference
    measurement   33-4
Asthma
    in small child   66-8, 70
    in thin child   115, 117
    see also Respiratory tract
    infections
Axillary hair   42, 128

Beam scales   32
Beckwith-Wiedemann
    syndrome   87, 101, 103
Blood pressure, and sex hormone
    secretion   131
Bloom syndrome   60
Body composition
    fetal   3

menarche and   122
    sex hormone secretion
        and   131
Body fat
    appearance, in growth
        hormone deficiency   105
    determination of   18, 98-9
    measurement and
        assessment   15, 99-100
    sex hormone secretion
        and   131
Body hair development   40-2,
    120-1, 128, 129-30,
    138
Bone age   see Skeletal maturity
Bowel disease, inflammatory, in
    small child   72-3
Brain growth   4-5, 13
Breast development
    gynaecomastia   88, 129
    as secondary sex
        characteristic   128-9
    staging   39, 41, 120-1
    in Turner syndrome   65-6

Caloric intake, in obesity   103,
    108-9
Cardiovascular disease
    in obesity   96-7
    in thin child   115, 117
Catch-up growth   19, 20, 74-6
Centiles   35-7, 44-51
    biparietal diameter   20
    body fat   15
    crown-heel, fetal   2
    head circumference   14
    height   10, 45, 57
    peak height velocity   11-12,
        121
    sitting height   57, 58
    skinfold thickness, triceps   56
    subischial leg length   58

Centiles (*cont.*)
  testicular volume 43
  velocity
    crown-heel, fetal 3
    height 10, 11, 47, 50, 67
    weight 114
Central nervous system
    examination, in early
    puberty 139-40
Cerebral and meningocerebral
    infections, in early
    puberty 140
Cerebral lesions and growth
    deficiency 73, 137
  in late puberty 145, 148-9
Chlormadinone acetate 141
Chromosomal mosaicism, in late
    puberty 150-1
Cimetidine 130
Coeliac disease 71, 115, 117,
    149
Contraceptive pill
  in late puberty 155
  in Turner syndrome 65
Craniopharyngioma 73-4
Crohn's disease 115, 117, 149
Crown-heel measurement,
    fetal 2, 3
Crown-rump measurement 1,
    31
Cryptorchidism 150, 155-7
Cushing syndrome 91, 100,
    101, 138, 142
Cyproterone acetate 141

Danazol 141
Decimal ages and dates 48-9
Dexamethasone 130
Diabetes
  in late puberty 149
  in obesity 97, 103
  in thin child 115
Dietetic advice, in obesity 108-9
Dihydrotestosterone 128
Down syndrome 101
Dysmorphism
  in late puberty 150
  in obesity 101, 102-3, 107
  in tall child 85-9
  in Turner syndrome 63

Emotional stress
  causing growth
    retardation 21-2

  in excessive tallness 83
  in gynaecomastia 88-9
  in late puberty 145, 148-9
Endocrine
  disorders
    in late puberty 148-50
    in obesity 100, 101
    in small child 60-1, 63-5,
      73-4
    in tall child 89-91
  influences
    on growth 23-7
    in puberty 122-31
Environmental influences
  on body fatness 18, 98-9,
    101, 109
  on growth 7, 19-23
  on height 22
Exercise and growth 23, 101

Facial asymmetry, in low
    birthweight 115, 116
Facial hair development 128
Familial likeness
  in low birthweight 62
  in obesity 18, 98-9
  in small child 55-6
  in tall child 85, 91-2, 150
Fat child *see* Obesity
Feet, disproportionately large 89
Fetal growth and development
  birthweight ranges 5
  body composition 3
  brain growth 4-5
  crown-heel, measurement 2, 3
  environmental influences 7
  genetic influences 5
  hormonal influences 7
  maternal obesity, and 6
  neonatal length
    measurement 4
  nutritional influences 6,
    19-21
  smoking and 6
  see also Low birthweight
    infants
Follicle stimulating hormone
    (FSH)
  ovarian response to 152, 154
  role in reproduction 123-4,
    127
  secretion, in pubertal
    onset 126-8

GNRH *see* Gonadotrophin
  releasing hormone
Gastrointestinal disorders
  in late puberty 149
  in small child 71-3
  in thin child 115, 117
Genetics
  control of pubertal onset 122
  in determining body
    fatness 18, 98-9, 101
  growth influence 5, 17-19
Genital development (boys),
    staging 39, 40, 121
Gestational age and growth
    assessment 2, 3, 5
Gigantism 87, 90, 142
Gonadal dysgenesis 129, 148-9,
    150
Gonadostat 125
Gonadotrophin releasing
    hormone (GNRH)
  deficiency, in late
    puberty 148, 151-2
  in pubertal onset 26, 124-8
  role in reproduction 123-4
Gonadotrophins
  basal level, assessment in late
    puberty 150, 151-2
  deficiency, in late
    puberty 144-5, 148-9
  in pubertal onset 26, 124-8
  role in reproduction 123-4
Growth curves *see* Centiles
Growth delay
  extreme 78-9
  in late puberty 145-8
  in skeletal maturity 66-9
Growth hormone (GH)
  deficiency
    idiopathic isolated 75-6
    and obesity 104-6
    partial 61, 76-7, 145
    in proportionate short
      stature 61, 63-4
    in growth spurt,
      adolescent 127, 130
  role in growth
    regulation 24-5, 106
Growth process, in normal
    childhood
  body fat 14-15
  brain size 13-14
  endocrine influences 23-7

environmental
  influences 19-23
  genetic influences 17-19
  height 9-13
  timing of events 16
  see also Fetal growth
Growth spurt
  adolescent 9, 11-13, 120, 127,
    130, 146
  mid-childhood 21
  prepubertal 11, 146
Growth velocity
  in growth delay 67-9
  increased 89-91
  low 69-73
    treatment 74-9
  in puberty 146
  in small child 59, 61, 63,
    69-73
  therapy, effects 64-5, 67-9,
    74-9
  in thin child 113-14
Gynaecomastia 88-9, 129

Hair, development 41-2, 120-1,
    128, 129-30, 138
Hands, appearance
  in pseudohypopara-
    thyroidism 107
  in Silver-Russell syndrome 62
Hashimoto's thyroiditis 90
Head circumference,
    growth 14, 34-5
Height
  adult, prediction of 18, 37-9,
    44, 91-2
  clinical assessment 53-9, 83-4
  in early puberty 135, 138, 140
  environmental influences 19,
    21-2
  genetic influences 17-18
  in idiopathic isolated growth
    hormone deficiency 75
  measurement 29-32
  metric conversion 48-9
  in normal growth 9-13
  and sitting height,
    relationship 31, 57
  and skeletal maturity 37-9
  see also Small child *and* Tall
    child
Height velocity 9, 10, 47, 50-1,
    118
  in growth delay 66-7

Height velocity *(cont.)*
  in growth spurt,
    adolescent 11–13
  in Klinefelter syndrome 87–8
  in late puberty 146–8
Human chorionic gonadotrophin,
    in pubertal induction
    152, 153–4
Hyperinsulinaemia and
    obesity 101, 103–4
Hyperprolactinaemia, in late
    puberty 149
Hyperthyroidism 90
Hypogonadism, in obesity 101,
    104, 106
Hypogonadotrophic
    hypogonadism
  in late puberty 150, 156
  in obesity 101, 104, 105
Hypothalamic obesity 103
Hypothalamo–pituitary–gonadal
    axis
  deficiency, in late
    puberty 145, 148–52
  in early puberty 137
  and increased growth
    velocity 90
  role in reproduction 122–8
Hypothyroidism 78, 138–9

Idiopathic isolated growth
    hormone deficiency 75–6
Inhibin 123, 127
Insatiable appetite 103
Insulin 25, 103–4
Intrauterine malnutrition 19–21

Kallmann syndrome 151
Karyotypes 147, 150–1
Klinefelter syndrome 87–8, 144,
    150, 151

Laurence–Moon–Biedl
    syndrome 101, 103
Leg, growth 106, 130
Lesions, intracranial, in early
    puberty 138–9
Leukaemia treatment, causing
    growth deficiency 73
LHRH, assessment of levels in
    late puberty 151
Lipodystrophic child 114, 116
Low birthweight infants
  body asymmetry 117

facial features 116
familial likeness 62
nutritional influences 19–21
and small child 60–3
and thin child 114–15
Luteinising hormone (LH)
  in pubertal onset 126–8
  role in reproduction 123–5
  testicular response 152
Luteinising hormone releasing
    hormone *see* LHRH

McCune–Albright
    syndrome 137, 139
Malnutrition, growth
    influence 19–21
Marfan syndrome 85–6, 89,
    115
Maternal obesity and fetal
    growth 6
Measurement techniques
    (anthropometric)
  arm circumference 33–4
  centiles, construction and
    use 35–7, 44–51
  head circumference 34–5
  height 29–30
  height prediction 37–9, 92
  instrument accuracy 32
  sitting height 31, 57–8
  skeletal maturity 37–9
  skinfold thickness 33
  supine length 29–30
  weight 32
Medroxyprogesterone 141
Melatonin 124–5
Menarche
  relation to body
    composition 122
  timing, in puberty 121, 125–6
  see also Puberty
Mental retardation
  in cerebral gigantism 87
  in early puberty 139
  and homocystinuria 86
  in obesity 96, 100, 101, 107,
    109
Muscle growth 131

Neonatal length measurement 4
Neonatometer 4
Neoplasms, malignant, in early
    puberty 142

Neurocutaneous dysplasias, in
    early puberty   139, 140
Neurofibromatosis   139
Neurosurgical intervention,
    resulting endocrine
    problems   74
Nutrition
    assessment   32-4
    fetal growth and   6
    growth process
        influence   19-21

Obesity, in childhood
    body fatness,
        assessment   96-100
    causes   101
    clinical syndromes   100-3
    correlation with adult
        obesity   97-8, 109
    diagnosis and therapy,
        summary   96
    in early puberty   136
    endocrine problems   103-7
    familial likeness   18, 98-9
    management   108-9
    mental retardation and   96,
        100, 107
    mortality and   96-7
Oestradiol
    in pubertal induction   154-5
    role in reproduction   123-4
    secretion, in premature
        thelarche   120, 129
    in utero-vaginal
        development   129
Oestrogen administration
    at menarche   125-6
    in pubertal induction   155
    in tall child   93
    in Turner syndrome   65-6
Orchidometer   42, 43
Overnutrition   21, 100, 101, 136
    insulin and   25
Ovulation   123-4, 126
Oxandrolone, and growth
        velocity   64

Panhypopituitarism   144
    obesity and   104-5
Parental height
    and small child   55-6
    and tall child   85, 91-2, 150
Peak height velocities (PHV)   11,
        12, 121

Phospate-losing rickets   71
Pituitary gonadotrophins   26
Poland's anomaly   60-1
Prader-Willi syndrome   101,
        102, 103
Prepubertal velocity   12-13, 146
Progestogens   65, 126, 155
Prolactin and growth   25, 129
    assessment levels, in late
        puberty   151
Pseudohypoparathyroidism   106
    hand appearance in   107
Psychological disorders, in thin
        child   115, 117-18
Psychomotor developmental
        retardation, in obesity
        102
Pubertal staging, examination in
        early puberty   138
Puberty
    endocrine influences   122-31
    genetic control of   122
    growth hormone, effects   106
    growth spurt, adolescent   9,
        11-13, 21, 120, 122, 127,
        131
    gynaecomastia   88, 89
    induction of   142, 153-5
    oestrogen
        administration in   65-6,
            93, 125-6, 155
    peak height velocities
        (PHV)   11, 12, 121
    physical signs   120-2
    sex steroid, effects   106, 154
    skeletal maturity and   122
    staging   39-44, 120-2
    timing of onset   120-2
    see also   Adrenarche,
            Menarche and Thelarche
Puberty, early
    diagnosis and therapy,
        summary   134
    pathological   137-42
        causes   137
        management   140-2
        physical examination 137-40
    physiological   134-6
        causal frequency   135
        management   136
Puberty, late
    diagnosis and therapy,
        summary   144
    pathological   148-55

Puberty, late *(cont.)*
    causes 148–50
    investigation of 150–2
    management 152–5
    physiological 145–8
        causal frequency 145
        treatment 147
Pubic hair staging 40, 42,
    120–1, 128

Renal disease, in thin child 115,
    117
Respiratory tract infections
    in late puberty 149
    in obesity 100
    see also Asthma
Reticuloendothelial system, in
    puberty 131
Rickets, phosphate-losing 71

Scoliosis, and obesity 103
Sex hormones
    role in growth 26
    secretion, in puberty 131
Sex steroids
    assessment of levels, in late
        puberty 152
    deficiency, in late
        puberty 148
    in growth regulation 25
    in pubertal induction 153,
    154
    in skeletal maturity 130, 140
Sexual characteristics, secondary
    development 128–31
Silver–Russell syndrome 62–3,
    115
'Simple' obesity 101
'Simple' tall stature 91–3
Sitting height 31, 57
    subischial leg length,
        relationship 58
Skeletal maturity 15–16
    adult height prediction 37–9,
        44–6, 91–3
    growth delay and 66–9
    in hypothyroidism 37
    pubertal onset and 122
    'simple' tall stature and 91–3
    steroid, effects on 68–9
Skeletal radiographs, in
    disproportionate short
        stature 80
Skinfold calipers 33

Skinfold thickness
    measurement 14–15, 33,
        70, 149
    in obesity 97–100, 108
    in thin child 118
Small child
    asthma and 66–8, 70
    clinical assessment 53–9
    crown–rump measurement 31
    diagnosis and therapy,
        summary 53
    differential diagnosis 54
    disproportionate short
        stature 79–80
    emotional stress and
        growth 21–2
    endocrine disorders 60–1,
        63–5, 73–4
    familial likeness 55–6
    gastrointestinal
        disorders 71–3
    growth delay and 66–9
    iatrogenic short stature 73–4
    low birthweight 60–3
    low growth velocity
        and 69–73
    oestrogen administration 65–6
    phosphate-losing rickets 71
    proportionate short stature
        syndromes 59–74
        treatment 74–9
    sitting height
        stature and 57
        subischial leg length,
        relationship 58
Smoking, fetal effects 6
Socioeconomic deprivation
    and small child 22, 70
    and thin child 115, 118
Somnolence, in obesity 100
Sotos syndrome 87
Spermatogenesis 123–4, 127–8
Stadiometer 29, 30
Standards, anthropometric
    measurement 35–7
Stature *see* Height
Steroid treatment
    growth and skeletal maturity,
        effects 68–9
    in extreme growth delay 79
Still's disease 69, 115, 117
Subischial leg length, sitting
    height relationship 58

Subscapular skinfold
    measurement   15, 33, 100
Supine length measurement   29,
    30

Tall child
    clinical syndromes   85-9
    diagnosis and therapy,
        summary   83
    differential diagnosis   84-5
    with dysmorphism   85-9
    familial likeness   85, 91-2, 150
    with increased growth
        velocity   89, 91
    'simple' tall stature   91-3
    treatment   93—5
Testicular volume   42-3, 94, 121,
    126-7
Testis
    cryptorchid   150, 155-7
    fetal   5
Testosterone
    in pubertal induction   154
    in pubertal onset   25, 127
    role in reproduction   123-4
    in sexual development   128-9
    treatment, in tall child   94
Thelarche, premature   129,
    134-5
    see also Puberty
Thin child
    causes   115-18
    clinical assessment   113-18
    diagnosis and therapy,
        summary   112
    management   118-19
    medically significant
        thinness   112-13

Thyroid gland, examination in
    early puberty   138-9
Thryoid hormones   25-6
Thyroxin, administration in
    hypothyroidism   78
Thyroxin deficiency   24
Triceps skinfold thickness,
    measurement   15, 33, 56,
    100
Tuberous sclerosis   139
Tumours, intracranial, in early
    puberty   140
Turner syndrome   63-6, 129
    and late puberty   144,
    150

Ultrasound, in prenatal growth
    assessment   1-2

Vagina
    discharge, in early
        puberty   120, 138
    growth and development   129
Velocity centile
    crown-heel, fetal   2, 3
    height   10, 11, 47, 50, 67
    weight   114
Vertebral column,
    development   106, 130
Voice breaking   130

Weight
    changes, in thin child   113-14
    in defining fatness   99
    measurement technique   32
Whole body asymmetry, with
    low birthweight   62-3,
    115, 117